Praise for

The Afterlife of Billy Fingers

"*The Afterlife of Billy Fingers* is an extraordinary example of extended after-death communication. It's one of the most powerful, liberating, and healing books on 'life after death' I've ever read. In fact, you may have a spiritual experience while reading it that will transform your beliefs about life, death, and the afterlife. I cannot recommend it highly enough to everyone who is grieving the death of a child, spouse, parent, or any other loved one."

— Bill Guggenheim, co-author of *Hello from Heaven!*

"Having read *The Afterlife of Billy Fingers*, this world appears more deeply drenched in the sacred, and death feels like an adventure to look forward to. In this quirky, luminous account of the conversation between an introspective artistic woman and her dead bad-boy brother, Annie Kagan and Billy Fingers manage to collaborate on a work of transcendent wisdom, irreverent humor and sublime beauty."

— Mirabai Starr, author of *The Interior Castle* and *Dark Night of the Soul*

"*The Afterlife of Billy Fingers* by Annie Kagan is a wholly believable story that never loses its grounding in the daily life we all know. The voices of the narrator and her deceased brother never strike a false note. This is not a story that asks you to believe anything, but simply to listen with an open mind and heart. I think you will find yourself transfixed."

— Rev. Susan Varon, ordained interfaith minister

"*The Afterlife of Billy Fingers* is one of the best books I've read on the subject of life after death. So much of what the author describes jives with my experiences of both being with dying people at the moment of their deaths and in two long, extended near death experiences I've had myself. The book strikes chords of truth again and again and again. The excellent writing and the story itself hold the reader's attention beautifully. Skeptics will keep reading to 'find out what happens next.' And whether you're a skeptic or a true believer, the book will powerfully engage you. Part of the book's premise is Annie's questioning whether her communication with Billy is real or her own craziness, and that mystery keeps us reading and seeking answers. We want to find out for ourselves what the source of this communication really is. Along the way, what Billy tells Annie is inspiring, enlightening, and insightful. The book works. It's a good read with an appealing and controversial message."

— Hal Zina Bennett, author of more than 30 books including *Write from the Heart* and *The Lens of Perception*

The Afterlife of Billy Fingers

How My Bad-Boy Brother Proved to Me There's Life After Death

Annie Kagan

HAMPTON ROADS

Cover design by www.levanfisherdesign.com/Barbara Fisher

Cover photo by Irving Cohen, edited by Justin Smith

Interior designed by StanInfo

Lyrics from Mahler's Eighth Symphony reprinted with permission from William Zauscher, YouTube, accessed September 6, 2008.

Hampton Roads Publishing Company, Inc.

Charlottesville, VA 22906

Distributed by Red Wheel/Weiser, LLC

www.redwheelweiser.com

Sign up for our newsletter and special offers by going to *www.redwheelweiser.com/newsletter/.*

ISBN: 978-1-57174-694-8

Library of Congress Cataloging-in-Publication data available upon request

Printed on acid-free paper in Canada

F

10 9 8 7 6 5 4

To S.M.
I will forever love you

To my brother Steve
The Super Royal Radiant King

CONTENTS

Part Three: From Soul to Spirit

FOREWORD

This fascinating book may initially surprise and baffle some readers. After all, the events it recounts may seem completely unbelievable and far beyond reality. Therefore, I am grateful to Dr. Kagan for asking me to write this foreword, because it gives me an opportunity to talk about one of my favorite subjects—the incredible world of the ancient Greek philosophers.

The average American will probably find Dr. Kagan's narrative of her other-worldly adventures with a deceased brother hard to believe. That is too bad, though, because the Greek philosophers who founded Western thought knew full well about the remarkable phenomenon she describes. In fact, Greek philosophers even had a name for the people who were somehow suspended between this life and the next life. They called such people "walkers between the worlds."

The walkers between the worlds had important social functions. As the early Greek philosopher Heraclitus put it, they "watch over the living and the dead." In about 600 BCE, one of the earliest of these figures, Aithalides, was reputed to be able to pass back and forth at will between the physical world and the afterlife world. In Ancient Greece, walkers between the worlds served functions that in modern Western society are carried out by individuals who have near-death experiences. Specifically, they were mediators, intermediaries, or messengers between the realm of the living and the realm of the dead.

The philosopher Menippus was another famous walker between the worlds. Menippus visited the afterlife dimension, returned, and then wrote a book about his journey. Menippus was sent back from the afterworld and charged with the task of monitoring what was happening among humans on earth. Then he would report back to his superiors in the world beyond to keep them apprised of humanity's progress.

Menippus dressed the part. He sported an incredibly long gray beard and wore a long gray cloak tied at the waist with a scarlet sash. He carried a wooden staff carved from an ash tree. He wore a strange hat inscribed with the signs of the Zodiac. He was serious about his mission.

The experiences Dr. Kagan relates are completely consistent with the kind of role walkers between the worlds played in antiquity. And that is no surprise to me. I think that such experiences are part of the collective psychological heritage of humankind—not artifacts of any one culture.

I suspect there are plenty of other people like Dr. Kagan. However, Westerners have developed an utterly false impression that experiences like hers are impossible—or even pathological. Hence, the many people to whom such things happen simply don't report them for fear of being judged or ridiculed. Accordingly, I salute Dr. Kagan for her courage in writing this book.

In 2006, I conducted a seminar on grief for professionals and hospice workers. A middle-aged businesswoman who worked for the organization asked me about something that happened to her when she was almost killed. She was severely injured in a car crash and left her body at the scene. She immediately saw an old man in a gray robe standing beside the road. The man had an extremely long gray beard, carried a staff, and wore an odd hat. And she felt he was there to carry her across to the afterworld. Incidentally, I hadn't mentioned Menippus or other walkers between the worlds during my presentation. The woman spontaneously related her experiences out of her own curiosity. I suspect such encounters have been with us for thousands of years and no doubt occur to quite a few individuals.

Dr. Kagan's thought-provoking account is an excellent example.

Dr. Raymond Moody

This is a true story. Some names, places, and other identifying details have been changed to protect individual privacy. The timing of some events has been compressed to facilitate the telling of the story.

ACKNOWLEDGMENTS

Thanks to my friends Steve Wander, Caroline Fierro, Brian Keane, Laura Stein, Bobbi Shapiro, Jessica Gormley, Anna Kiersnowska, Eve Eliot, Cathy Gandell, Ruth Washton, Sophie LaPaire, and Pamela Millman.

Gratitude to my book angels, Dr. Raymond Moody, Mirabai Starr, Elise D'Haene, Katharine Sands, Hal Zina Bennett, Howard Kaplan, Stacey Donovan, Michele D'Ermo, Teresa Kennedy, Ashley Womble, Jillen Lowe, and Sallie Randolph.

Thank you Deena Feinberg for my author photo, Justin Smith for his magic on Billy's cover photo, and William Zauscher for permitting me to use his magnificent translation of the lyrics to Mahler's Eighth Symphony.

Blessings to Barbara, Danielle, and Samantha from Poppy Bill, and to the rest of the crew, Mems, Rocco, JimBob, Leslie, and Steven.

Special thanks for joining me on this odyssey to Michele Tempesta, Ann Patty, Claire Gerus, Jill Mangino, Tex, Stephen Gorad, my publisher Jan Johnson and the team at RWW, and to the Cherry Boy, je t'adore.

All my love to my family: my mother, Florence, whose dark beauty and goddess-like strength have taken up residence as the lioness of my heart; my father, Irving, my handsome, charming Rhett Butler, who always looked at me like I was the greatest miracle on earth; and Billy, my bad-boy-Buddha-brother.

Part One

Still Billy

Dear Annie,

Every need a Book Dedicated to them.

Read Between the Lines.

Luv
Bill

ONE

The First Thing That Happens

The Miami Dade Police left a message on my answering machine at nine in the morning. "If you know William Cohen, please contact Sergeant Diaz at 305 . . . "

Oh no! Billy must have been arrested. Not prison. Not again. Not this late in his life.

It still made me queasy to think about the time my brother was arrested almost thirty years ago; the thud of the gavel, the words "twenty-five years to life," my mother crying in my arms, begging the judge to change his mind. The day I watched the police handcuff Billy and drag him off to Sing Sing for selling cocaine was probably the worst day of my life.

I was shaking when I punched in the phone number of the Miami Police.

"This is William Cohen's sister. Has he been arrested?"

"No," Sergeant Diaz said in a soft voice. "He was hit by a car at two-thirty this morning. I'm sorry. Your brother is dead."

My heart went cold. Dead? My head spun. I was dizzy. I reached for a chair and sat down.

"What happened?"

"William was coming from the emergency room at South Miami Hospital. He was drunk and ran out onto the highway," the sergeant reported.

"Were you there?" I asked.

"Yes, ma'am. I was called to the accident scene."

"Was Billy injured?" *Injured? What am I thinking? He'd been run over by a car!* "I mean, was he taken to the hospital?"

"No, ma'am. Your brother never knew what hit him. Died instantly. Didn't suffer at all."

Died instantly? Didn't suffer? How on earth could he know that? The sergeant was trying to cushion the blow, but it wasn't working.

"William was wearing a hospital ID bracelet. We got your name and phone number from their records."

So that's how they found me! Billy always wrote me in as his "in case of emergency" person.

Sergeant Diaz cleared his throat. "Listen, ma'am, you don't have to identify the body. The bracelet is good enough. Better to remember him as you do now."

Better to remember him as you do now? Oh my God!

The sergeant must have heard me start to cry, because the next thing he said was, "It's kind of against regulations, but if you give me your address I'll send you the things your brother had on him."

Since I didn't have to view Billy's post-accident body, there was no reason to fly from New York to

Miami. By the time my sixty-two-year-old brother died, he was homeless, so everything he owned was in his pockets. My brother had left things neat and tidy for me—not like when he was alive. What I had worried about for years had now happened. Billy was dead.

I called Billy's drug counselor at South Miami Hospital. Eddie's voice was edgy.

"Billy showed up at the ER last night, high and coughing up blood. He wanted to be admitted to the hospital so when the nurse told him he'd have to go to the detox unit instead, he got belligerent, picked up a chair, and threatened her. She called the cops, Billy ran out, and, you know the rest. Your brother just didn't trust his Higher Power. I'm really disappointed in him."

Disappointed? Billy was dead. And Eddie was *disappointed?* I hung up on him and threw the phone across the room to get his words as far away from me as I could.

Oh God, Billy is dead! My body ached so much I felt like I was the one who'd been run over. I got into bed with my clothes still on and pulled the covers over my head. Then I remembered the incredibly strange thing I'd done the day before.

Although we hadn't spoken in months, for the last week I'd been thinking obsessively about Billy. This was unusual because trying *not* to think about Billy was a survival tactic I began practicing in fourth grade. As a little girl, I adored my big brother, but

I was always afraid something terrible was going to happen to him. Billy was constantly in trouble. I didn't really know what "trouble" meant, but when the trouble got bad, he would be sent away to some mysterious place. And when the trouble got really bad, my parents didn't even know where to find him.

In fourth grade my parents explained that the trouble Billy was in was something called "heroin addiction." To distance myself from my anxiety, I began practicing the art of cold-heartedness.

All these years later, the week before he died, no matter how cold-hearted I tried to be, I couldn't stop thinking about Billy. Living alone in a small, secluded house on the Long Island shore and working at home didn't help. I tried to distract myself from my angst by keeping to my routine—up by six, feed the cats, meditate, walk by the bay, make lunch, go to work in my music studio writing songs.

Sitting at my electric keyboard, all I could think about was Billy. I wanted to phone him, hear his voice, tell him I loved him, help him in some way. But I didn't know how to reach him. Part of me was afraid to reach him. I was sure he was in bad shape.

The day before Billy died, a bitterly cold January morning, I layered on two sweaters, a down jacket, and two wool hats and ventured into the raw air. I walked across the frozen brown leaves, through the bare winter woods, and climbed down the wooden staircase that led to the bay. I never ask God for favors, but that morning I looked up at the silvery sky, raised my arms, and imagined pushing Billy into the hands of the great Divine. "Take care of him for me," I whispered.

Hours later, Billy was dead.

The next few days I stayed in bed, unable to do anything but drink tea. They say there are different stages of grief—shock, guilt, anger, depression. But all those feelings collided and came crashing in on me at once.

My friend Tex stopped by to see how I was doing. "It's weird," I told her. "It's not like I'm sad, exactly. I feel like a voodoo doll with pins stuck in me everywhere."

I had given Tex her flashy nickname because she was five-foot-eleven, dark-haired, angular, and partial to cowboy boots. Even though she looked tough, she was kind and always thought about what she said before she said it.

"Oh, honey," Tex said, taking my hand, "That's grief." Tex would know. She lost her older brother, Pat, in a plane crash when she was just a teenager.

Three days after Billy's death a monster storm moved through Long Island. I pushed the foot of my bed up against the window and watched the blizzard tear up the world outside. Billy loved wild, turbulent weather, and as the storm obscured everything, I felt a kind of satisfaction. The snow was "whiting out" my world, just as death had "whited out" Billy's. I've always believed something exists beyond death, but what that something was, I had no idea. As the wind screamed through my windows, I was sure it was Billy's spirit, making his usual racket, knocking around the sky, trying to find his way.

The storm passed and the winds subsided. I spent my days mostly in bed, crying. The rest of the time I was swallowing Valium until I was a walking zombie. My long, dark, wavy hair was lank and uncombed, my eyes puffed into slits, my skin haggard. I didn't look forty-something anymore, I looked a hundred—and that was okay with me, because every time I saw myself in the mirror the verdict was always the same: guilty.

Over the last few years I had done everything I could to help Billy: hospitals, rehabs, psychiatrists, methadone clinics. Nothing worked. His struggle became a black hole that sucked me into his chaos. I came down with a different ailment every other week and saw one doctor after another. Finally, I pleaded with him, "I can't take this anymore! Please stop calling me!" But he didn't. He couldn't. Then, instead of talking, we were mostly crying and screaming at each other. One day he did stop calling. And now he was gone.

Three weeks of post-death misery and self-recrimination later, it was my birthday. Just before sunrise, as I was waking up, I heard someone calling my name from above me.

Annie! Annie! It's me! It's me! It's Billy!

It was Billy's unmistakable deep, mellow voice. I was startled, but not at all afraid. In fact, I felt comforted.

"Billy?" I said, half asleep. "You can't be here. You're dead. I must be dreaming."

You're not dreaming. It's me! Get up and get the red notebook.

Suddenly, I was very much awake. I'd completely forgotten about the red leather notebook Billy had sent me last year for my birthday. I was touched that he had made the effort to send me a gift even though he was becoming overwhelmed by his addictions.

I jumped out of bed and found the red notebook on a shelf in my bedroom closet. The pages were blank, except for an inscription written on the first page.

> *Dear Annie,*
> *Everyone needs a book dedicated to them.*
> *Read between the lines.*
> *Love,*
> *Billy*

What a strange thing for Billy to have written! *Read between the lines?* I ran my fingers over the familiar handwriting. Then I heard him again.

It's really me, Annie. And I'm okay, it's okay because . . . I grabbed a pen and wrote what he was saying in the red notebook.

The first thing that happens is bliss; at least it was like that in my case. I don't know if it's that way for everyone who dies. As the car hit me, this energy came and sucked me right out of my body into a higher realm.

11

I say "higher" since I had the feeling of rising up and suddenly all my pain was gone.

I don't remember hovering over my body or looking down on it or anything like that. I guess I was pretty anxious to get out of there. I knew right away I was dead, and went with it, more than ready for whatever was waiting.

I wasn't aware of traveling at any particular speed. I just felt light and unburdened as the sucking motion drew me up inside a chamber of thick silvery blue lights. People who have near-death experiences sometimes say they went through a tunnel. I'm using the word "chamber" because a tunnel has sides, but no matter what direction I looked, there was nothing but light for as far as I could see. Maybe the difference is I had a one-way ticket and theirs was a round-trip.

And even though I didn't have my body anymore, it felt like I did and that it was being healed. The lights in the chamber penetrated me and made me feel better and better as they pulled me up. It wasn't just the wounds from my car accident that were being healed. In the first nanosecond that the lights touched me, they erased any harm I suffered during my lifetime: physical, mental, emotional, or otherwise.

Soon, Daddy appeared right there beside me, young and smiling and handsome as ever. He was making jokes and asking, "What took you so long?" It was so great, seeing Daddy, but I'm guessing he was there to be a familiar landmark in foreign territory. I'm saying that because he was only with me for part of the ride and Daddy definitely wasn't the main event.

The main event was the silvery lights and their party atmosphere. Those healing lights had a festive feeling, like they were cheering me on, saying, "Welcome home, Son."

I can't say how long I was floating up the healing chamber, because I no longer have a sense of time. But I can say that chamber was some kind of cosmic birthing canal that delivered me into this new life.

I want you to know, darling, there's nothing hard or cruel for me anymore. I glided from the chamber right out into the glorious Universe. I'm drifting weightlessly through space with these gorgeous stars and moons and galaxies twinkling all around me. The whole atmosphere is filled with a soothing hum, like hundreds of thousands of voices are singing to me, but they're so far away I can just barely hear them.

And although I can't exactly say anyone was here to greet me, as soon as I came out of the chamber I felt a Divine Presence; a kind, loving, beneficent presence, and really, that was enough.

In addition to the Divine Presence I also feel beings around me—Higher Beings, I guess you would call them. I can't explain why I'm using the word "beings," and not the singular; I just know there's more than one. I can't see or hear them, but I can feel them moving about, swooshing by, doing different things that concern yours truly. And although I haven't got a clue what these things might be, I'm guessing that floating out here in space is euphoric instead of terrifying because I'm being attended to by this celestial crew.

I'm looking down on the earth, and it is down. It's like there's a hole in the sky, a hole between our two worlds,

I can look through and see you. I know how sad you are about my death. Sad is too small a word. Bereft is more like it. But death isn't as serious as you think it is, honey. So far, it's very enjoyable. Couldn't be better, really. Try not to take death too seriously. As a matter of fact, try not to take life too seriously. You'd enjoy yourself a lot more. That's one of the secrets of life. You want to know another secret? Saying goodbye isn't as serious as it seems either, because we will *meet again.*

As suddenly as it came, Billy's voice dissolved. I was sitting on my bed, the red notebook resting against my knees, its first pages filled with Billy's words in my handwriting. Had I just imagined his voice? Maybe. But where did these words come from? They definitely weren't mine.

Inside the front cover of the notebook I found a card my brother had sent along with it—a cartoon of a big orange tomcat hugging a girly little purple kitten. The card's message was uncanny. *Are you real or am I dreaming you?*

Was I having some weird dream-like grief reaction? How could I know? I couldn't, and at that moment I didn't really care. For the first time since Billy's death I felt happy . . . more than happy. Billy was okay. And as he described floating blissfully through the stars, the atmosphere of his world had somehow flowed into mine. I was almost euphoric.

And all of a sudden I was hungry. I got out of bed, went to the kitchen, and made a pot of tea. As I sat at the table gorging myself on biscuits and marmalade, I opened a magazine. Staring at me was an ad for White Cloud bathroom tissue. It featured a cloud with a piece cut out that made it look like a hole in the sky. Hadn't Billy just said he saw me through a hole in the sky? I got chills. Maybe the ad was some kind of sign.

"That's ridiculous," I told myself. "I really *am* going a little mad." But some part of me wondered if there really might be a connection.

Are you real or am I dreaming you?

Everything was so strange but it all fit together—Billy's appearance, the forgotten red notebook, its inscription, the card's message, the picture of a hole in the sky. And before I heard from Billy, I was so depressed I could barely raise my head off the pillow. Now, I felt completely serene.

Had Billy appeared just this one time to let me know he was okay? Was that the end of it? I hoped not. If he visited a second time, I would be ready. I would be objective and alert so I could figure out if he was real. I decided to lure him back by keeping the red notebook and a pen with me all the time.

TWO

Still Billy

I decided not to tell anyone about Billy. Ten years ago, when I was taught how to meditate on the light within, my teacher instructed me to keep my spiritual experiences to myself; otherwise, I might lose them. Hearing from Billy in the afterlife was a spiritual experience, wasn't it? If this was real, it wasn't something I wanted to risk losing.

Five days after my birthday, as the sunrise cast my white bedroom into shades of rosy pink, I heard Billy's voice again. Blurry-eyed, I reached under my pillow for the red notebook, propped my head up, and started scribbling.

Hey, Princess. Good morning.

When Billy was alive, his calling me "Princess" was never a compliment. From the beginning, my life seemed charmed compared to his, and he held that against me. Billy was a "problem child"—and I was a "little angel." I sang and danced in school plays— he tried to sing in a band but couldn't carry a tune. Billy flunked out of high school—I was a straight-A student. The better I did, the worse he looked, and felt. Feeling guilty, I tried to win his affection, but that was something I couldn't succeed at.

Was Billy now using the nickname "Princess" because he was still holding a grudge? It didn't seem like it. The light that came along with his voice filled me with love.

I like the idea of you, or me, writing a book. I think maybe I should get permission, but I'm floating in space and there's no one to ask. No one, that is, except the invisible Higher Beings I mentioned before, and I don't want to disturb their benevolence by asking for favors too soon [laughs].

I never got permission for anything in life. That's because it was a different deal. Those in power here should be in power. Not like on earth. There's such a lack of kindness on your planet.

It's hard to be kind all the time where you are, because if you don't toughen up, you go under. The nature of existence there is harsh. You fix one hole and another pops up. It's supposed to be like that, though, so don't be too concerned about it.

I was done with my life, Annie. I paid my debt, although it's not what we usually think of as payment. It wasn't some price for my so-called sins. It was more a learning thing.

How do I know my life wasn't some punishment for my past transgressions? Well, because there's no such thing. You're not on earth to be punished. It's not about sin and punishment. That's a human concept. Something man made up. Humans make up stuff and then they believe it.

Sure, there's a lot of pain in life, but not because you've done anything to deserve it. Here's another secret for you, baby sister. Pain is just part of the human experience, as natural as breath or eyesight or blood moving through your veins. Pain is part of the earth deal, so don't be overly concerned about it. Although I admit I wasn't exactly fond of pain myself.

And how do I know all this? Honestly, I don't know. All of a sudden I know a bunch of things I didn't know when I was alive. When you're born, when you pop out, that big pop gives you a kind of amnesia. One of the main things we're doing when we're alive is trying to remember the things we forgot.

There's a different kind of knowledge here. You're really understood, and what a relief that is. So many problems in life come from not being understood or known. People on earth sometimes get glimpses of each other's souls, like when they fall in love. The difference is, here, I am my soul. I'm still Billy but without my body.

I imagine it could be hard for some people, not having a body. When you realize you just died, with all the mumbo jumbo you've heard on earth about what might be waiting for you, I guess you could be feeling apprehensive. Not me. I dove into being dead. Felt right at home.

I know, my sweet sister, you're wondering if all this is just a figment of your imagination, something your mind made up to help you feel better about my recent departure from earth. How will you know the reality of this? Well, because I will give you evidence—let's call it proof—so you will know for sure this is not your imagination and that it's really me, Annie. It's Billy.

And do something for me, Miss Greta Garbo. Give Tex a coin.

While Billy was speaking, I understood everything he said. But after his voice faded, I couldn't remember a single word. Once again, Billy had put me into a state of euphoria. Communicating with his soul had caused my own to open up, and the whole world was changed. I no longer cared about being objective. Billy had returned. That was all I cared about. I lay down for a while to concentrate on my breathing and ground myself a bit.

After that, I went downstairs, lit some logs in the fireplace, and tried to re-orient myself. My mind threw out a barrage of questions: Was this really happening? Why was I able to hear my dead brother speaking to me? Had I just gone through some kind of out-of-body experience? I didn't think so. I hadn't traveled off somewhere. The somewhere had come to me.

I opened the red notebook and read over what I had written. It sounded like Billy, at his wise and charming best—Billy when he was clear and sober.

And he seemed to be able to read me. He knew I doubted that he was real.

Suddenly, it didn't seem logical that I was having delusions. Delusions don't acknowledge your doubts. Maybe the Billy phenomenon was like a phantom limb, something that seemed as though it was still there even though it wasn't. Or maybe I was hearing his voice inside my head, like when someone says, "I can hear my father's voice in my head telling me . . ."

Only this voice wasn't *inside* my head—it was *outside*, and it sounded as if I was standing at the bottom of a long staircase and he was at the top. Both times I'd heard him, he was above me and to the right.

Even more strange was that he had told me to give my friend Tex a coin. Why? How did he even know her name? He'd never met Tex. And now he wanted me to tell her about him. All my life I did things for Billy I didn't want to do—lie to my parents, give him money, let him crash on the sofa in my tiny apartment for weeks at a time. Did I still have to do what he wanted now that he was dead?

The thought of telling Tex about Billy made the magic of his dimension fade. As my mood fizzled, the mundane world seemed even more mundane than before. But still, something exciting had happened. Something way beyond my routine, everyday existence.

Three years before, I'd come down with a bad case of world-weariness. Maybe almost a decade of serious meditation had made me too detached from the highs and lows of normal existence. From the outside my life looked pretty good—a successful career as a chiropractor in New York City, a husband who was a partner in a law firm, and a songwriting collaboration with a talented music producer. But in a matter of months, everything fell apart. My husband, Steve, suddenly seemed like a stranger, working with patients gave me migraine headaches, and I hadn't sold a single song.

The only thing I was sure I wanted was solitude. Hence, Billy's nickname for me: Greta Garbo. So, feeling as if I was jumping off a cliff, I separated from my husband, sold my practice, left the city, and moved to an old house on the tip of Long Island.

I bought some used sound equipment and put together a music studio. I'd written songs since I was a teenager and had come close to selling a few to major recording artists. It seemed far-fetched, but if I devoted myself to music, maybe I could make a living as a songwriter.

For six months, alone by Gardiner's Bay with my two cats, I made demos of songs that no one bought, meditated three or four hours a day, took long walks by the water, and sometimes saw no one but the postman for days.

But even solitude has a way of getting to you. After a week of not wearing anything but pajamas, and letting my hair get so dirty it looked like a tossed salad, I decided to join a local writers' group. Maybe I had a novel in me. I didn't believe I was suddenly going to become a bestselling author, but it got me out of the house.

That's how I met Tex, the leader of my writing group. She had published a memoir and written some episodes for a popular cable TV show. We liked each other from the start.

But why had Billy told me to give her a coin?

I took out the manila envelope Sergeant Diaz had sent me after Billy's death. It contained his few remaining possessions: a beat-up address book, a key card from a Ramada Inn, two pairs of dirty glasses, a torn leather business card holder, and seven dollars and change. Was this all that remained of my brother's life?

I spread the change on my kitchen table. What coin was I supposed to give Tex? A quarter, a nickel, a dime? Just then, I heard Billy's voice.

Find . . . my . . . car.

That shook me up. This wasn't like hearing Billy's voice while still in bed, half asleep—I was in my kitchen in the middle of the day. And his voice was louder—robotic and commanding. I got scared. This wasn't something I could handle by myself anymore. Even though we were separated, I called my husband, Steve.

"I have something really weird to tell you." I took a deep breath. "Billy's been talking to me."

"That's wild! What does he say?" I could tell by his tone he was giving me the benefit of the doubt.

"I've been writing it down." There was silence on the other end. "You don't think I'm crazy, do you?"

"No." Steve assured me. "People don't go crazy all of a sudden. Something's going on. Fax me the pages."

That was Steve. Get right down to business.

"There's more," I said. "Just now I was in the kitchen, and I swear that Billy told me to find his car. Did he even have a car?"

Steve was able to answer that question because he was the only one who'd stuck by Billy until the day he died. Whatever my brother needed—money, advice, friendship, compassion—Steve always came through.

"Billy had an old Mercedes he was living out of," Steve reported. "But he drove it into a tree a week before his death. It's probably in some junkyard in Florida."

So Billy did have a car! "I'll call you back," I told him, and hung up.

Even though I was shaken, I needed to know if Billy was still around and if he'd answer my questions. I looked up at the ceiling and asked out loud, "How can I find your car, Billy?"

My . . . card . . . holder.

Barely breathing, I pulled the cardholder from the manila envelope, and found a business card from a Mercedes dealer.

Get . . . the . . . things . . . from . . . my . . . car.

"What things?" No answer. "What things, Billy?" He was gone.

Trying to sound composed, I called Hans, the Mercedes dealer whose name was on the business card I now had in hand. I almost fell down when he told me that he did have my brother's wreck! Either I had suddenly become psychic or Billy actually was communicating with me. When I asked Hans to send Billy's things, he said he'd do it right away.

The next few mornings, as I woke up, I whispered Billy's name, but there was no sign of him. In a way I was glad I couldn't conjure him up. He was in charge of this affair. He was the responsible one . . . for a change.

THREE

The Divine Nature of All Things

A few days after Billy's kitchen visit, I saw Tex at my writing group. Every Wednesday evening, from seven to nine, a small group of aspiring writers sat around the huge gray stone fireplace in Tex's living room and read our new chapters out loud. Since most fledgling writers secretly believe they're writing the next bestseller, we were very mild and sensitive in our critiques. But after class, Tex and I sat alone and mercilessly dissected the readings of the night. We weren't being cruel. It was how she was teaching me to write.

After class that night, Tex, as usual, downed glasses of scotch. I sipped Pellegrino. When she was at the bottom of her second glass, I said, "Want to hear something outrageous? Billy's been talking to me."

She blinked, but at least she didn't laugh.

"I'm not kidding. And I've been writing it down. Do you think I'm nuts?"

"So, that's it," she replied. "You've been miserable since Billy died. But tonight you're lit up. Yeah, I believe it. Why not?"

"Billy said he wants me to give you a coin, but I have no idea what he's talking about."

Tex smiled. "I like it. I like that he wants to give me something."

I took out a photo of Billy I had slid into my purse.

"Dark and handsome," Tex said, "He looks like he has a secret no one else knows. I'd go out with him. I mean, I would have."

I'd heard that before. Women were charmed by Billy. It's not that he had to try; it was his special gift.

"What does he talk about?" Tex asked.

"Bliss, light, invisible Higher Beings."

"I think you should read it in class next week," she said.

"Are you kidding? I'm not letting people know my dead brother's talking to me. Besides, I'm not supposed to speak about my spiritual experiences."

"Think of it this way. These are Billy's experiences, not yours. You should read it," Tex insisted. "Pretend it's a new novel you're working on. Billy's the main character and he's talking to his sister from heaven."

"I'll think about it."

Maybe it was a leftover from when he was alive, but I didn't want anyone judging Billy and his new circumstance. Even though I was much younger than him, all my life I'd felt that Billy was a misunderstood child and I was his protector.

Maybe this time I was the child and he was the protector. Either way, it seemed too risky to read his words to my writing group. I was afraid they'd all think I had flipped.

The next time Billy visited I planned to ask him if I could read his notes in class. Two days later, when he woke me before dawn, my question vanished into the light of his dimension.

Good morning, baby sister.

Even though I don't have my body anymore, I do still feel like an individual. So much for disappearing into a sea of bliss. Don't misunderstand. I'm deep into the bliss experience, but I definitely haven't disappeared.

What is bliss? Bliss is like being in love multiplied by a thousand, but it has nothing to do with anyone else. It's fulfilling in and of itself. On earth you usually need someone to give you a reason to feel love, and that feeling usually has its ups and downs. With bliss, there's no downside—and you don't need a reason for it. As your soul floats through this dimension, it's just natural to feel bliss.

The kind of bliss that exists here isn't compatible with the human body because bodies are subject to certain laws. I'm sure there are laws here too, but they seem very lenient, easygoing, inclined in your favor. There's a lot of freedom going on here that you don't have where you are. Earth, the conditions there, traps you in limitation. For me, there seems to be no limitation, only potential.

That's because God, or Spirit, or whatever you choose to call it, is undeniable where I am. As I drift through space, the light rays from the celestial bodies that sparkle all around me, well, those rays have a personality of sorts—qualities, like wisdom, kindness, compassion, and intelligence. Sometimes I believe the light rays are actually the super-thoughts of a Supreme Being. Other times I think they are the Supreme Being itself. I can't really say.

Being in an earthly body and looking through physical eyes limits the way you perceive the light. Your eyes can't see the light directly, only the things it shines upon, so the light remains invisible, just like the soul does. That causes a good deal of suffering down there on your planet because it's hard to believe in what you can't see. The light here makes visible what is invisible on earth: the divine nature of all things.

The best cure for suffering? An enlightened experience of it all. What does that mean? It means finding the invisible within the visible. You are not only the person who walks the earth. You have a soul. And that's what the spiritual search is about.

And Princess, even though I disappointed you in the past, don't dwell on that. Disappointment is part of the pattern of earth. But things change. I know you've heard this a million times, but it is a secret. Things change. When you die, you realize how much and you realize there are immortal things, things you take with you, and they change too.

The Eastern concept of Maya, or illusion, what does this mean? It means temporary. It means our lives are temporary.

The next Wednesday night, writing group night, was cold and blustery. As I walked up the stone path from my car to Tex's house with the red notebook in my bag, the floodlights seemed brighter, the moonlight more silvery, the bare trees more sculptural.

"The Billy effect," I told myself. It was the first time I used that phrase.

Six of us settled into Tex's nubby gray couches and chairs. I was the first reader that night.

"I've started a new novel. It's a little quirky." I took out the red notebook and read Billy's first two entries.

When I finished, I looked around the room and saw nods of approval. Maybe they were being kind; everyone knew my brother had just died.

Only one person—J.B.—hadn't looked at me. I knew he wouldn't be kind. J.B. was cool, distant, and unemotional. Also, we had an unspoken competition about who could find the most flaws in the other's work.

Tex just sat there, staring into her coffee cup, waiting.

Suddenly, I felt an irresistible pressure and couldn't keep quiet. "The truth is, I know it sounds crazy, but Billy's been talking to me. What I just read really came from him."

"Then you have to write it like that," said Tex.

"Writing a book with my dead brother? It's too weird." I scrambled to explain my reluctance. "You guys already know me. But people are going to have a lot of opinions about this. They'll think I'm a spaced-out ditz, or worse, a fraud."

"Since when do you care what people think?" asked Tex.

"I don't care. I just don't want them to ruin it for me."

"There's a Brazilian author," J.B. said, "late nineteenth century, Machado de Assis. He wrote a great book called *The Posthumous Memoirs of Bras Cubas*. The main character is dead and he's speaking from the afterlife. So do what you did with us. Pretend it's a novel. No one ever has to know."

I went to sleep that night hoping Billy would visit in the morning. But days passed without any further sign. Maybe I'd lost my spiritual experience by talking about it. Why had I listened to Tex instead of my meditation teacher?

This time I was the one who'd disappointed Billy, not the other way around.

FOUR

They Can't Take That Away from Me

Two weeks after I read his messages in class, it was Billy's birthday. I still hadn't heard from him and was feeling blue. When I woke up in the middle of the night, my whole body hurt.

Billy's probably upset with me, probably feels I've betrayed him, exposed our secret. Why hadn't I asked for his permission? Oh God, listen to me! I've become an airy-fairy weirdo who needs permission from her dead drug addict brother. I'd better get my feet back on the ground. Billy probably isn't even real.

Then, I heard Billy—singing.

No, No, they can't take that away from me . . .
Don't worry, Princess. Even though I left the earth, you haven't lost me, have you? I'm kind of your guardian now. I don't blame you for having doubts about all this. But if I'm not real, how come my singing makes you feel so much better? Especially since I still sing out of tune [laughs].

It's an energy I bring you. It's love. Not earth love. Not dependent on what you do or how you look. Not

31

the kind of love where today I hate you and tomorrow I love you, although it's usually the other way around. It's usually more like yesterday I loved you, but today I hate you because you're not who you were the day before. I bring the kind of love that exists where I am.

How come? I guess it's being allowed. An exchange between us, between different dimensions. Why? Maybe because I want so much to give you something, and this is something you're able to take. You need another dimension in your life, Miss Garbo.

You're calling on me because it's my birthday, but I'm in deep learning and it's hard to talk even though you want me to—and I'm sorry about that. Why don't you bundle up and walk by the bay? The salty blue living water, the snow on your face. Turn to nature to pardon some of the difficulty you have to bear. Nature has more light than anything else on your planet. Then, instead of your usual meditation, think about the healing chamber I went through when I died. It's the part of the afterlife that touches your body at death, so it's not far from your world. I know when I described it you could feel it a little.

Got to go. Happy birthday to me.

When it got light outside, I put on my winter gear and headed for the bay. Just as I arrived, a light snow began falling. The water, the sky, the chanting of the gulls, and the gentle dance of the snowflakes all heightened my sense of exhilaration.

So Billy was my guardian now. My messed up big brother was leading the way. He knew things about me he didn't know when he was alive. He knew I meditated. He probably also knew that I had stopped since his death.

When Billy died, I was too wrecked to sit on my yellow silk cushion in the corner of my bedroom. I tried to meditate while lying down, but all I felt was pain. Pain instead of light. For the first time in ten years, I'd close my eyes and nothing would happen. I couldn't find the light inside me.

The bitter wind coming off the bay got to me and I headed home. I lay down on my bed, closed my eyes, and tried to imagine being inside the healing chamber. Soon, I felt silvery light surround me like a spotlight. My cells began twinkling like tiny stars as the light pulled these stars upwards, out the top of my head and into itself.

When I got up, I felt as if I'd just showered in a waterfall of pure energy. Instead of feeling the light inside me, I was now inside the light. I remained in that state of bliss for hours, drinking tea, eating by the fire, composing at my keyboard. My eyes were open the whole time, eyes open.

After the chamber experience, I was able to meditate again. I'd sit on a cushion for hours in a darkened room, focused on the inner light. When you meditate for hours at a time, you hit walls, you get uncomfortable, your mind annoys you, and you're dying to stop. But you stay with it and break through.

Now, with Billy's help, I was also breaking through in a different way. My brother, my crazy, unpredictable, charming big brother, was telling me the secrets of the cosmos. It was the most unexpected thing that had ever happened to me. I had no idea when Billy would visit again. There was no pattern, except he seemed to prefer sunrise.

FIVE

Ain't No Sunshine Without the Sun

A few days after Billy's birthday I received a call from the insurance company of the driver who ended Billy's life. The insurance guy told me that when the car hit my brother, his head went through the windshield, from the outside of the car, and that Billy had come face to face with the driver. Whatever he said after that was a blur. When we hung up, I put my head down on the desk and cried. Soon, Billy's soothing voice came through the ceiling. I grabbed the red notebook.

So you're having a bad morning and I'm sorry about that. My head going through the windshield was a detail you didn't need to know, Princess.

What an angel that driver was! What a saint! To go through all that to deliver me! I needed to be delivered, darling. I wish you could find that guy and give him a kiss for me.

And of course today is the Ides of March; the anniversary of the day I went to jail for selling drugs. I was never a major league drug dealer. I wasn't even in the minor leagues; I was just trying to make enough money to keep my own habit going. The life of an addict is not an easy one. It's a very particular road, but it was just part of my road.

Head through the windshield. Dealing drugs. Jail for a few years. Nothing you would be interested in, but it was interesting to me. How far out on the edge could I go before I would fall off?

I fell off, Annie, and it didn't feel that good. Not really. Not when I had just turned sixty and my charms were fading.

Remember all the women I was blessed to have love and care for me along the way? Women really like that particular combination, the bad-boy-saint. And that's kind of what I was, a pure-hearted spirit burning up in the fire of life, an undercover agent from the angel squad, a dark messenger of light.

I had that bad-boy-saint thing going on, and on top of that I needed saving. Women love "the redeeming your soul" thing. And okay, I was dark and good-looking with a deep voice that was the icing on my particular cake. I had the right voice with the right words sifting through it because no matter what, I was always sincere.

How could I be so beautiful and so terrible at the same time? The truth is, I don't know!

And when you go to your writing class tonight, Annie, give J.B. a message. "There ain't no sunshine without the sun." Say it where you read how I got hit by the car.

"You must be kidding. I'm not giving that message to J.B.," I said out loud.

J.B. was the last person in the group who'd want to hear from my dead brother. I was already risking looking like a nut case, reading Billy's communications in class; now he wanted me to deliver a personal message to the most skeptical person in the group. I was sure J.B. had suggested I turn Billy's notes into fiction because he believed that's what they were—fiction.

"There ain't no sunshine without the sun?" Maybe Billy meant the lyrics "Ain't no sunshine when she's gone," from the old Bill Withers song.

Ain't no sunshine without the sun, Billy repeated out of nowhere.

"So you can read my mind. Big deal. I'm still not doing it!" I said back.

That night, to my surprise, after I finished reading about Billy going through the windshield, I turned to J.B. and said, "I know this sounds weird, but Billy wants me to give you a message: 'There ain't no sunshine without the sun.'"

No one, including J.B., had much of a reaction.

Then it was J.B.'s turn to read. He was writing an autobiographical novel based on his time in France. Quite unexpectedly, while reading, J.B. choked up and began to cry as he described an event none of us knew about—his young son had been hit by a car and killed.

The room went silent. J.B. stopped for a minute, then started reading again. Like everyone else, I was shocked and saddened. Then it hit me. It isn't S-u-n, it was s-o-n! There ain't no sunshine without the *son!*

When J.B. finished reading, no one said a word. He was the last reader of the night, and as soon as he finished, he quickly gathered his papers and left.

I stayed after class and Tex brought out the scotch. "Did that really just happen?" I asked.

"Oh yeah," she said, smiling her fetching crooked smile. "It definitely did."

"And Billy told me to say it right where he talked about his accident. Did anyone else get that? The car accident thing?"

"I don't know, Annie. I don't know about anyone else, but I was thinking there's no way Billy's message to J.B. could be a fluke. It was too specific, too dramatic. I wonder what J.B.'s thinking?"

"Maybe, in some strange way," I said, "Billy was trying to let him know his son's soul still exists."

I got into bed that night feeling excited and afraid, like a kid riding a roller coaster. My heart was pounding. Something important had happened, and the fact that there were witnesses to that something seemed to up the ante. Until now, some part of me was still doubtful that I was really talking to Billy. The skeptic in me wasn't sure that my subconscious wasn't just personifying my brother to help me cope with my grief. But what happened in class was too amazing to write off as pure coincidence.

When I woke up the next morning with a swollen face and an excruciating toothache, my excitement from the previous night turned to pure fear. I never should have delivered that message to J.B. Was I transgressing some boundary between the living and the dead? Maybe my punishment was a toothache, a warning not to go any further.

Why should I be doing things Billy tells me to do? When he was alive, he hadn't exactly been an authority on what could get you into trouble. Was he as dangerous in the afterlife as he had been in life? But I knew Billy loved me, and would never do anything to harm me. Would he?

SIX

Hologram

After my toothache and the painful root canal and awful infection that followed, I was scared. I wanted answers. Every morning I waited for Billy to show up and give me an explanation, but there was no sign of him. He was gone. I couldn't believe he engineered the crazy event with J.B. and then disappeared. But that was Billy. Just like old times.

Billy's message to J.B. convinced me I wasn't just imagining his communications. But who was I to be the one to prove there's life after death? Maybe some secrets shouldn't be revealed. Maybe I was breaking a sacred taboo, dabbling in a cosmic Pandora's box.

I missed the next writing class because of my tooth. I was glad when Tex told me no one had brought up Billy's message. Instead of keeping it with me, I put the red notebook in the drawer of my night table. It was nearly a month later, in early April, before Billy showed up again.

Good morning. I didn't abandon you, Annie. I hate to tell you this, but you're not the only thing on my schedule, Princess. So you got scared because you had a toothache. No, darling. That didn't happen because you're doing

41

something wrong by talking to me. The Divine forces aren't punishing you for writing about what happens after you die. I told you, there's no such thing as that kind of punishment. Don't stop writing our book just because you got a toothache.

You're so sensitive. That's one of the reasons we can have these communications. You were always such a sensitive child, the one with all the fear. Well, maybe if I had myself for a big brother, I'd be scared too [laughs].

After our last visit, I was drifting through the Universe, taking in the sights, when a cosmic wind began to circle me like a slow tornado. This wind contained some kind of magnetic force because white crystals gathered around its edges like snowflakes on a car windshield. When the whirling stopped, the crystals had formed a ring around me. This ring seemed to be about thirty yards from me. I say "seemed" because there's no way to measure real distance. It could actually be light years away.

Then it was like someone pressed the start button on a cosmic projector and the ring became a circular movie that's still playing all around me.

What I'm looking at is very different from any film I've seen in a theater, though. First of all, I'm suspended in the middle of the Universe, and second, the entire movie is playing all at once and the images are holographic.

There are an uncountable number of multi-dimensional, true-to-life images circling me: a baby screaming in his crib; a dark, curly-haired six-year-old leaping from rooftop to rooftop while his mother yells at him from the sidewalk; a teenager in black jeans with a cord wrapped around his arm; a guy in a suit kissing a gorgeous blond in a wedding chapel in Las Vegas. It doesn't take long to recognize that I am the star.

When we're alive, there's something inside us, a sort of cosmic computer chip, that records everything we go through. Right now, I'm watching my whole life from my birth to my death. I'm looking here, looking there, fast-forwarding, rewinding, zooming in and out. I see the paths I took, and the ones I didn't. I see where my genius was, and where I might have done better. I don't feel moralistic or judgmental about any of it, though. It all just seems interesting.

What's really great is that this hologram has a very special feature. You know how you sometimes think to yourself, "What if?" For example, when I was alive I often wondered, "What if I had married my first love?" or "What if I had done well in school?"

Well, guess what? My hologram is expandable. I can live out the life those "what ifs" would have brought me to. I can follow all the different paths I didn't take when I was alive and see how they would have turned out. What's surprising, though, is that it doesn't seem like one way is more valuable than any other. I don't have a preference. It's all fascinating, and I have no regrets.

I know that must seem strange. I did a lot of things that most people would call mistakes, big mistakes. But the way I look at it, I had a great life. It was all great, even the hard parts.

Of course, I didn't see my life that way when I was alive. My new viewpoint takes the difficulty, the struggling feeling, out of it all. That's because even though I'm very much aware that it's me up on the cosmic screen, I'm watching it from a distance, so all the ups and downs, all the dramas, seem like they're happening to someone else.

It's funny. They say there's Judgment Day after you die, but actually the opposite is true. There's No-Judgment Day. Viewing my life has become surprisingly enjoyable because I have an absolute acceptance of myself and everything I've done. It would have been nice if I'd been able to have this attitude when I was alive, but I guess I wasn't that advanced. You'd have to be like the Buddha to be that advanced.

Everything looks so much better now than it did then. It's like I'm on some kind of drug. It's not like any drug I've ever taken, though. It's very pure and much more wonderful and there are no side effects. Oh, and it's not illegal [laughs].

I think this so-called drug is really the Divine Presence and its immediate relatives, those Higher Beings. Why do I say this? Because at this point there's no question in my mind that there are Beings in the atmosphere around me: wise, kind, super-evolved Beings whose loving custody I'm now in. And remember, when you think about love, you're using your human mind. There's no comparison to the actual over-the-top nature of this love.

I guess when you receive real love, when someone loves you unconditionally, I guess you begin to feel that way towards yourself. Unconditional.

As Billy spoke, I was again swept into the light and energy of his world, and forgot my concerns. Hours later, when the effects were wearing off, dealing with the minutiae of everyday life wasn't easy. Like an astronaut, I was having trouble readjusting to gravity. That earthly pull was weighing me down. I felt like a dysfunctional alien not suited for living in this world.

That afternoon, while I was in my kitchen, Billy whispered:

Show me the money.

By now he'd figured out that whispering made hearing from him in bright daylight less jolting.

Call Tex and say, "Show me the money."

I assumed that phrase referred to the as yet unidentified coin my brother wanted me to give her.

"Tex," I said when she answered the phone, "Billy wants me to tell you, 'Show me the money.' Does that mean anything?"

She was silent for a few beats, then laughed.

"I took the dogs to the ocean this morning. I was thinking about Billy." Tex paused. "Actually, I was talking to him. I'll keep what I said between him and me, but I asked him for a sign. I wasn't even going to tell you about it."

I waited while Tex took a drag from a cigarette.

"I came home, took a shower, then, okay, this is weird . . ."

"Yeah."

"Well, I was thinking about my novel, dancing in front of the mirror with a towel, saying over and over, 'Show me the money. Show me the money.'"

Now I went silent. Tex was laughing, but I was more confused than amused. This wasn't just about my hearing Billy's voice, which was strange enough. Billy's conversations with me were one thing, but now Billy was bringing other people into his realm—Tex and J.B. and my writing class. Why?

SEVEN

Rescue Mission

When Billy woke me a few days later, he was speaking so quickly I couldn't keep up. "Hold it," I said out loud, putting the red notebook aside. "I need my computer. I can't write this fast."

My computer sits on a desk in front of tall sliding glass doors through which I can see treetops and a lot of sky. Now that I was sitting in a spot filled with natural light, Billy's voice had an even more magical feel. I could look through the bare branches at the sky, which is the direction his voice comes from, and watch the Billy effect make the world luminous.

Good morning, darling. Let's fill in a bit of the story that brought us both here. All I have to do is zoom to that part of my hologram. Don't worry. I know the rescue mission was a nightmare, but I'll make it entertaining.

Well, first I disappeared—what, about five years ago? I went to Margarita Island, that jewel in the crown of Venezuela, to make my fortune running a sports betting operation. Bill Cohen became Billy Fingers, a name I picked to commemorate the accidental amputation of the tip of one of my fingers while I was working in a wedding band factory when I was sixteen. You remember—the accident that introduced me to my first taste of the world of pain relief.

Five years ago, Bill Cohen got tired of feeling like a taxi-driving ex-junkie mascot of his designer wife's entourage of wealthy friends. Without much planning, he said goodbye to his beautiful wife and their million-dollar co-op on the Upper East Side of Manhattan and ran away to Venezuela to become Billy Fingers. I ran away from home, just like when I was a kid running away from Mommy.

Although in my younger days Mommy was always the one who bailed me out of trouble, our relationship was difficult from the day I was born. That's the thing about human beings. They're not just one side of the coin.

Actually, the whole thing between Mommy and me started even before I was born. Soon after Mommy got pregnant with me, she started to bleed. She bled so much she began thinking I was trying to kill her from inside her womb. So she developed this kill-the-baby-before-he-kills-you kind of attitude.

The doctors prescribed bed rest—complete bed rest—and injections to calm her down. In those days, they didn't know that it wasn't so great to give a pregnant woman morphine. Morphine can make unborn babies develop a taste for it. So you could say I was getting high back there in the womb.

Anyway, I ran away to the tropical shores of Margarita, with my scheme to get rich quick. But things didn't turn out the way I planned.

Now that I'm dead, I see the whole drama that led to the rescue mission. I see you on the beach near your house that day in June, three years after I had disappeared. You were sitting on a blanket, looking out at the ocean, wondering what had become of me. You were also thinking, "It's probably better that I don't know."

Then you closed your eyes and had a dream of sorts. You dreamed I was walking along the horizon, slow and tired. My spirit was rising up, big and magnificent, out of my tattered old body. You had a searchlight in your hands, and sent a beam across the ocean to buoy me up. It was one of those dreams that feels like it's really happening. Now that I'm dead, I can see it all.

By the way, after you die, when you watch your hologram, you get to see everything—who loved you, who hated you, what they did for you, and what they did to you when your back was turned. As I said before, you spend a lot of time viewing what you did on earth, so be sure to make it interesting.

And here's another secret for you, my sister. There is no right way for things to turn out. Some endings are happier, some not so happy, but it's not just the happiness percentage that matters. It's the music of it. Most people's lives don't have enough music. I was lucky; my life was a rock opera.

After you dreamed you sent that beam across the water to your sick, old, stoned-out brother, what did I do? I called Mommy the next day. Even though I had been missing for years, Mommy, in her inimitable nurturing style, told me never to call her again and hung up. She had quite a way with me, Mommy did. It felt like the good old days.

Now that I'm dead I know that Mommy called you, hysterical and guilt-ridden, to confess how miserable she had been to me on the phone. I caused Mommy a lot of pain in her lifetime, that's for sure. Desperate, I called her again a week later and she gave me your number.

Thank God my baby sister would still talk to me. Wanted to, even. That smart, pretty little brunette thing in the pink tutu singing and dancing and getting all A's while her brother, Billy the Kid, was setting fire to the school cafeteria.

You were so happy to hear my voice on the phone after all those years, even though I was stoned and crying and itching. I was already in hell and the next stop was going to be even lower. If I didn't leave Margarita Island soon, I was going to wind up in jail or a loony bin, some place I'd never get out of.

You wired me money for a plane ticket, but I spent it on other things.

I really wanted to get out of there, but I didn't have the wherewithal to act like a normal person and get myself on a plane. Everyone told you I was indulging myself, but you suspected something more serious was going on.

I wasn't happy that Billy had started talking about the rescue mission. Maybe he was zooming in on it with his newly enlightened after-death perspective, but remembering it was still painful for me.

While Billy was falling apart in Margarita, I was lying in bed in a state of Billy-induced malaise. I had trouble focusing on anything other than waiting for his next call, which came every few days, sometimes every day. Each time he was in an even worse state than the last time I'd spoken with him.

"Annie. I'm dying. I'm itching to death. I'm having anxiety attacks. You've got to get me out of here."

"How can I if you won't tell me where you are, Billy?"

"I don't know where I am. All I know is I'm itching. Don't let me die here like this!"

I looked to various advisors for answers—a psychotherapist, a drug counselor, people in Alcoholics Anonymous. The consensus was that Billy was manipulating me to get money for drugs. He could come home if he wanted.

Then I dreamed that my father came down from heaven and was digging a hole in the shape of a coffin. He dropped his shovel on the ground, turned toward me, and shook his head like he was troubled. His face was mournful and filled with misery, warning that something really dark was going to happen, something worse than death. When I woke up in a sweat, I knew it was Billy's grave he was digging and I had to get him out of Margarita, fast.

EIGHT

First the Pleasures, Then the Pestilence

Thinking about the rescue mission made me anxious. That night I kept waking up from crazy dreams, just as I had when Billy was trapped in Margarita.

In the morning I went to Starbucks for a double espresso. The sun was shining and the air carried a welcome hint of spring. As I drove home, a piece of sky seemed to turn a brighter shade of blue. Then I heard Billy's voice coming right through my windshield from that same bright place.

Call Tex and tell her I said to drink green tea.

It was the first time Billy had spoken to me when I was outside my house. I might have been scared if there hadn't been a light beaming down on me from the bright patch of sky with a familiar intoxicating effect.

Call Tex now. Drink green tea.

I reached Tex on her cell.

"Billy just gave me another message for you. 'Drink green tea.'"

Tex's gasp was audible.

"I'm coming from the acupuncturist. He said I'm toxic and have to stop drinking coffee. You know me

53

and my coffee. I was just this minute thinking, 'How in the world am I going to do that?'"

After I got off the phone, it hit me. Billy's cryptic messages—Ain't no sunshine without the son, Show me the money, and now Drink green tea—were the "proof" Billy had promised. These inexplicable incidents were his way of proving to me that he was real.

When I got home, I went straight to my computer, and looked out the glass doors up at the sky.

"Okay, Billy. I get it. You're real. But can you tell me how you were able to make these proofs happen?"

As always, I had no control over what Billy said.

Hello, my sister. To tell the truth, if it wasn't for the itching, I never would have called you from Margarita. I was having too good a time, at least up to that point.

At that time I was making money, collecting money. In one of the toughest enclaves of Margarita Island, Bill Cohen, a Jewish boy from Brooklyn, got guys to pay up their gambling debts. Hard to believe, huh?

We're meant to engage in all kinds of things on earth— things that don't make sense from a human point of view. So take a moment before you judge your fellow man too harshly. A lot of people judged me, but I was dealing with circumstances I had signed up to explore before I was born.

I was living with lovely young Elena. Elena was maybe twenty, and I was—what, almost three times her age. Sweet Elena took me under her soft little wing.

I never really liked drinking that much, but at that point I didn't have money for drugs. I let myself drink as much as I wanted, let the whites of my eyes turn yellow, let my teeth get rotten. I didn't care about the conventions anymore, or the future or the consequences.

First came the pleasures, then the pestilence. Nausea, anxiety attacks, hair falling out in clumps. And then the best one—the itching. Unbeknownst to me, these scabies were burrowing under my skin. I was so anesthetized from all the drinking it took me a while to feel the itching, and by then the bugs had gone so deep the town doctor couldn't identify them. They moved from area to area, doing their own special little dance.

In all my years I never experienced anything as harsh as these bugs. Were they God bugs or Devil bugs? Good bugs or evil? Is it all the same? I can't say, but for sure it was the itching from these bugs that made me call home, and I now know that if I had stayed in Margarita, the underworld had some very special treats in store for me, some very personal designer bon-bons the likes of which I'd never seen. Most of my life I got away with it. From other people's points of view, things didn't always look like they were going so great for me, but to me it was an interesting adventure. Like I said, I had signed up for it.

What I was getting into in Venezuela was another story. The darkness had me cornered.

It was your love and determination that snatched me from that fate. You were my hero. Lots of people had strong opinions about your attempts to save my life. They tried to assign you various roles that weren't particularly flattering. The pitiful victim, the codependent—and, my personal favorite, the fool—for trying to save an addict *like me. I wish I could have told you then, but I'm telling you now. To me, you were the grace of God, pure and simple.*

Here's another secret for you, honey—some more big brotherly advice direct from the other side. Don't be overly concerned about how you look in the eyes of others. People will pretty much see you as they will. Play your part in the cosmic drama, but never forget, baby, that you choose the way you see yourself. Don't let others do the casting.

When Billy was in Margarita, visions of being abducted and held for ransom in South American drug country had made my going to find my brother out of the question. After two months of trying to convince Billy to get on a plane and leave Margarita Island, and desperate to make myself feel better, I had gone to see Olga, the Colombian manicurist, to have my toenails painted red.

"What's wrong with you?" she asked. "You look like hell."

I blurted out the story. She's tough, Olga. She thought for a few minutes and said, "I know a guy—a really big guy. He can go find your brother. For a price."

I stared at her. A sort of kidnapping. How fantastic! Why hadn't I thought of that?

The Colombian guy wanted ten thousand dollars to find Billy and bring him back. Now that my wheels were in motion I happened on a better solution.

I could send my good friend and fellow meditator, Guru Guy, the Jewish boy from the Bronx, who was the king of South American travel.

"I'm sending someone to get you, Billy."

"No! Really? I can't believe it. Oh my God, hurry up! I'm dying. This is no way to die. Itching to death."

"Tell me where you are and he'll come get you."

"I can't, Annie. I can't."

"Why not? You're driving me crazy. I can't take this anymore."

"I can't come home, Annie. I look awful. My hair's falling out. I'm all bloated. My flesh is hanging, like Daddy's when he was dying of cancer."

Now I understood. Billy had always been good-looking. He was still vain.

Finally, the itching won out over Billy's vanity. The plan was for Guru Guy to fly into Margarita. Billy would somehow get to the airport, they would take the same plane right back to Miami, and I would meet them there. If Billy was a no-show, Guru Guy would start the search.

NINE

Billy-Dust

Now that the weather had started to warm, I began thinking I should do something with Billy's remains. His ashes had been sitting in a rosewood box by my fireplace for almost three months.

When Billy was alive, he always said he wanted to be cremated and scattered in the sea. I suddenly had the impulse to take his ashes to the bay across the street from my house so they would be close by.

I put on white clothes like they do in Eastern funeral rituals. After I poured Billy's remains from the box into a red silk embroidered purse, I sifted through the light gray speckled ashes with my fingers. Billy-dust. There were small, hard white chunks in it, probably bone, and a large piece of metal that looked like part of a dental bridge. I slipped on a jacket and went to the bay. The sky was intensely blue and cloudless, and the wind was blowing in the right direction, out to sea.

When I put my hand into the ashes, a piece of sky got brighter, and I heard Billy's voice.

It's too cold for me, honey.

"What?" I asked.

It's too cold. The water's too cold.

I stood there, not sure what to do. "You know, you could have told me that before I came down here."

Tell you what. Just sprinkle a little bit so you can feel like I'm here.

As I threw a handful of his ashes into the sea, Billy said:

The world is your oyster
The world is your oyster
You are the pearl
And the oyster

I had no idea what that meant, but it made me feel luminous. When I returned to my house, I could still feel Billy around, so I sat down at my computer.

Thanks for sprinkling some of my ashes in the bay this morning. I feel better. I really do, though, because you did it with so much love.

When I was alive I used to say my life ended the day you were born, and I'm sorry for that now. It's just that I was always the bad one and you were the good one. And Daddy loved you so much! It was one thing if Mommy loved you more than me, but not Daddy, too. The family drama is the first one, the primary one, and it has a lot of oomph. My envying you was a major factor in that drama.

On earth there's a lot of who's-better-than-who-type issues and that causes a lot of suffering. It's a game devised by the forces of Maya, or illusion, to make people unhappy. That's one of the purposes of illusion: human misery.

But the way I see it from this side of things, every soul is unique in very beautiful ways. Some are just farther along the path of development than others, and that's okay.

Now that I'm dead, I know it was no fun being the good one, always having to clean up the family mess— and we were messy, that's for sure. And I was the one who got all the attention, wasn't I? It was always all about me. What a revelation that was!

But you always loved me anyway, didn't you? Took your first steps to me, wrote little rhymes for me, looked up to me and out for me like I was your own personal James Dean. And what did I do? I pretty much ignored you. Well, that's over now. I'm making up for lost time.

The blessing I gave you today? It's more than some reward for what you did for me. It's a thing of the spirit. Infusing your life with it is the outcome of this moment and all it contains.

I can see you sitting at your computer right now, crying. You're crying because of how it ended between us. I struggled with my addiction for almost two years after the rescue mission; then I died. You rescued me, but couldn't really rescue me. It was written. Those last few months before my death, you told me to stay away and leave you alone. I was a drowning man, Annie, taking you with me.

I don't care much about memories anymore, but when I see you sitting there, crying, I want you to know there are memories much bigger than the fights you and I had at the end, down there on that very temporary planet. Memories like getting on that plane from Margarita with my new sidekick Guru Guy, crashing in a motel room in Miami, then waking up from my intoxicated sleep and seeing you standing over me like a Madonna. I had been away such a long time and I was so happy to see my baby sister, caring for me, saving me, getting me ready for the hospital, doing whatever it took to keep me from dying in hell.

So now you're crying at your computer, wondering if I forgive you.

Maybe the real question to ask yourself is, do you forgive me?

And really, darling, there is no one to forgive, because we signed up to do this dance together before we were born. We weren't acting out some type of I-did-something-wrong-to-you-in-another-life-and-I'm-paying-for-it-now kind of thing. It doesn't really work like that. That concept of an eye for an eye, tooth for a tooth karmic equalizing of the score isn't the real deal, at least not where I am.

It's more a kind of experiment chosen for soul-type reasons that humans have an almost impossible time understanding. And not understanding is an important part of the experiment. If people knew the workings of the experiment, it would lose some of its punch, and that losing of punch, well, that's a little bit of what enlightenment is all about.

TEN

Vincent

After his pearl in the oyster blessing, I wanted to give Billy a special tribute. The next day I decided to spread his remains in the Catskill Mountains in Upstate New York, a place he always loved. The year before his death he'd promised to take me on a trip there to see the autumn leaves.

I packed the red silk purse that held his ashes in my overnight bag, drove for five hours, and checked into a small hotel-spa I had stayed at before. It was a bare-bones, funky place, but the pine trees and forest were spectacular. I ate lunch, dressed in white again, put the silk purse in a backpack, and walked up a large hill.

When I reached the top, a big buck with huge antlers was staring at me from the edge of the trees like a mythological forest guardian. A little scared, I approached him slowly and stopped about fifty feet away.

"May I scatter Billy's ashes in your forest?"

When he didn't attack me but ran off into the woods, I thought that meant it was okay. At the spot where he had been standing, I opened the red silk purse. Then I heard:

It's too lonely here. And it's not cold now, but it's freezing in winter.

"I just drove for half a day, Billy. Why didn't you stop me?"

Billy didn't answer, but I could feel his spirit everywhere, like a bright mist illuminating the hills. I walked back to the hotel with the ashes still in my backpack. The shabby buildings looked like enchanted cottages, and people's faces were glittery and beautiful. I decided to stay until lunch the next day and scheduled a morning massage with someone named Vincent.

Before Billy escaped to Margarita, he was a masseur, one of his better gigs. I never met anyone with hands as gifted as Billy's. Another reason he liked the name Billy Fingers.

When I woke up at daybreak in my dimly lit room, my brother was waiting.

Thank you for honoring me by carrying my ashes to these sacred mountains. The miracle of creation is here in this place, everywhere: the trees, the skies, the sun, the friendship, the kindness, the love. Perhaps today I can give you a small sign, a small miracle, a small thing of beauty that will connect you to the source of all beauty and miracles.

Vincent turned out to be a big, round, twenty-something guy with slicked back blond hair and phenomenal hands. I don't know if it was because of

64

the similar feel of their touch, but while Vincent was rubbing my back with warm oil, I told him about Billy. I didn't care if Vincent thought I was a weirdo. I'd never see him again. When the massage was over, I pulled the sheet around myself, sat up and saw that Vincent was crying.

"My sister died a few months ago. She just got sick and died, all of a sudden, like that. She wasn't even twenty. Thank you so much for sharing your story about Billy. I think that you're, you're like some kind of sign from her."

I was taken aback. This was the first time I had told a complete stranger about Billy, and he didn't think I was crazy. He thought I was a messenger.

"Yes," I agreed, remembering Billy's message that morning. "It must be a sign."

Walking from the spa to my small, musty room, the woods and sky were humming with the Billy effect. Billy must have had something to do with my meeting Vincent. Did Vincent's sister have something to do with it too?

As I ate a bowl of chickpea soup in the restaurant before heading home, Vincent came to my table. He handed me a tiny round red straw basket with three crystals inside. Vincent explained that the clear quartz was for the mind, the rose quartz for the heart, and the rare dark red citrine was for the blood, as in brother and sister.

ELEVEN

More Proof

After I returned from my trip to the Catskills, I told my writing group about Vincent. When I admitted that sharing my Billy experience with a stranger had been more a gift than torture, Tex gave me her I-told-you-so look.

The next morning was misty. As the late April showers turned the earth fragrant and green, Billy showed up sounding lazy, his words softly drawn out.

Tell . . . Steve . . . lead . . . us . . . not . . . into . . . temptation.

I phoned Steve at the office to deliver the message.

"Billy just gave me a message for you. 'Lead us not into temptation.' What does it mean?"

"It doesn't mean anything," he said. His voice was clipped. "Listen, I have a meeting and I'm late. We'll talk later."

I was surprised. This was the first time my brother had missed the mark.

A few hours later Steve called back.

"In the middle of my meeting, one of my partners told a story, and the punch line was . . . Lead us not into temptation. He repeated it twice. I almost fell off my chair. I guess any doubts I had about your brother are gone."

After Steve hung up, Billy gave me another clue.

Tex . . . Bach . . . flower . . . remedy . . . clematis.

Bach flower remedies are a kind of homeopathic treatment for emotional distress. I speed-dialed Tex.

"Did you ever hear of Bach flower remedies?"

She laughed. "Yeah."

"What's so funny?" I asked.

"I'll tell you after. Go on."

"Well, Billy wants you to take one called clematis."

"Just yesterday, my sister said I should take a Bach flower remedy. I'd never heard of them before. Now Billy's prescribing one? This is wild."

Tex and I went online and searched clematis. It was for people who prefer to live in a dream world rather than reality. That fit Tex to a T.

"Billy wants me to know he's watching me," said Tex. "And watching out for me."

Twenty minutes later, Billy gave me another prescription.

Lola . . . Bach . . . remedy . . . vervain.

Lola was Guru Guy's girlfriend. Both of them had been following the Billy story, so I immediately called Guru Guy and delivered the message. He called me back minutes later.

"I just gave Lola Billy's message and guess what? She was at a health food store looking through the Bach remedies when I called. Guess what else? She had a vial of vervain in her hand."

These proofs, coming all on the same day, made me feel like I was in a wonderland—an invisible reality that Billy was making real for me. I put on a yellow slicker and drove to a nearby fishing village, then sat on a weathered wooden bench, looking out to sea.

It was July when I'd last seen Billy. We were sitting on this same bench, drinking coffee and eating donuts. Guru Guy had rescued him from Venezuela the previous summer and Billy had come up from Florida to visit. When we went into a donut shop, he ordered for me. I was surprised that he remembered I liked vanilla icing, rather than chocolate. I loved being near my big brother, watching the waves roll in. Now, though, sitting alone in the rain I sensed his presence all around me.

Part Two

Even the Soul Changes

TWELVE

Becoming the Universe

Billy went silent for a while, though sometimes I could feel him around as I went about my day. It was almost June when he visited me again, but he sounded very different. His voice was slow, hypnotic, and dreamy, and seemed to be coming from far, far away.

I know my voice sounds funny today—far off and kind of intoxicated. Don't get scared, little one. I'm not high [laughs]. I'm just further along than I was before. I'm alone, but it's a good alone, not like the alone I felt those last years of my life.

After you die, you spend a lot of time, solo time, exploring yourself as a Universe. Do you believe that? You are the Universe. But society teaches you different. Society teaches limitation. Believe me, Annie, everything you ever need is already inside you. And who you really are is far beyond your comprehension. That's why living squeezed into the human experience can be painful at times. It was for me.

It's been, what, about four months since I was hit by God's delivery service?

I thought I'd never get tired of watching my hologram. But after a while it became clear that all roads ultimately led me to the same place—the present moment, floating out here in space, which is a lot more fascinating than looking back at the life I left behind. My hologram must have had some built-in destruct mechanism, because as I lost interest in it the images faded to nothing.

As the last image evaporated, out of nowhere this super-radiant vertical ray of blue-white light burst onto the scene. The light beam was about ten times my size (I don't really have a size, but you know what I mean) and reminded me of a stick figure zigzagging like a wavy electric current. Coming out of its body were a bunch of fluorescent branches that looked like arms reaching in my direction. This light seemed friendly, glad to see me. I felt friendly toward it, too, but since I had no idea what the proper protocol was I didn't say or do anything. I figured I wasn't the one in charge.

You're probably curious about why I felt friendly toward a giant figure with lightning tentacles, but the benevolence of whoever or whatever this was left no room for fear. I'm pretty sure it was one of those invisible Higher Beings who's been hanging around. Maybe I'm only ready to meet it in this form. Or maybe this is its form. I can't really say.

What I can say is that the Higher Beings seem to be particular attributes of the Divine Presence. This Presence—the limitless light that fills the Universe everywhere—its personality contains every good quality imaginable. Perfect wisdom? Yes. Tender compassion? Of course. All-encompassing love? Definitely. Whatever qualities come under the heading of benevolence, that virtue is right there in the light. It's different with these Higher Beings. They're more specific, more personal, like the Divine Presence is focused through a prism. And the colored rays that come through the prism—these are the Higher Beings.

Anyway, as the lightning-type Being came closer to me, it radiated an electric kind of energy right through its phosphorescent arms. I compare it to electricity not because it was painful in any way but because it gave me a jolt. The kindness and understanding from the Higher Beings now comes to me from myself. I love myself as I never could have when I first arrived in the afterlife. I guess that means even the soul changes.

If there's one thing worth doing on your planet, it's discovering self-love. I say "discovering" instead of "learning" because learning implies you're starting from zero; but the truth is, you already love yourself. When you're born, when the amnesia happens, you forget your magnificence, and think you have to earn the right to be loved. How can you earn what already belongs to you?

My encounter with the Light Being began a new phase of my journey, the phase I'm now in: becoming the Universe. That electric jolt made me rise up, spread out, and expand across the cosmos. I've got stars and moons and galaxies inside and around me. There's some kind of processing happening, like there's a giant pinball machine of light waves inside me, and the sensation keeps getting better and better.

The thing about becoming the Universe is—and I'm going to say this but the words aren't really going to do it justice—the more I let go of my so-called self, the better I feel. As I blend more and more into the Universal energy, I think, "This is it, I'm going to lose myself." But it feels so good I don't care, so I let go and blend. Then, lo and behold, I'm still myself, but more blissed out. That's why I sound so dreamy.

Becoming the Universe is how I understand the incomprehensible nature of this otherness, how I venture into a dimension of what you may call the Source. And I can say, most inadequately, that at the center of everything is an energy, an immaterial material that for lack of a better word I'll identify as love. Wow, baby sister, and how I love and how good it feels, this love. You can't imagine it. You really can't. There is no way for you to.

I guess that ordinarily someone going through this isn't talking about it, just experiencing it, but who knows? Who knows why you can hear me? After I died, I could see you and I could see all that pain in you, and I started to talk to try to make you feel better. It was a big surprise that you could hear me. I'm as surprised as you are. And speaking of surprises, one is coming.

I was having a hard time hearing Billy. He sounded like someone slowly coming out of anesthesia or waking up from a deep sleep. Although his voice was faint, the euphoric feeling that his words carried with them was stronger than ever.

I took a blanket and some pillows and spread them on the deck outside my bedroom. It was a breezy morning, and the moon was still visible. Could what was happening to Billy up there happen in some way to me down here?

I wanted to become the Universe, like my brother. Staring at the vast, cloudless blue sky, my confusion about what to do with my life began to dissolve. Maybe I didn't have to be a particular someone or something. Maybe I could let go of all the ways I define myself. Maybe it was okay for things to be just the way they are.

My reverie was disturbed by the phone ringing. It was someone asking permission for my meditation teacher to use two of my songs on a program to be aired around the world. Years ago, I'd sent my teacher a CD of my songs, but I'd never expected anything to come of it. What a surprise! Billy was right, again.

I was filled with questions. How does Billy know what's going to happen? How far into the future can he see? Can he see my whole life? Can he influence what will happen? Is Billy simply some super-psychic part of myself? The questions seemed to loosen the earth's gravitational pull on me. I felt like the air.

THIRTEEN

Two Universes Passing in the Light

My moodiness returned the following morning, but mood swings were a price I was now willing to pay. I couldn't wait to hear from Billy again. Days passed with no sign. Was he gone? Had his voice become so faint that it was impossible for me to hear him?

Ten days later, at dawn, I saw an oval-shaped blue light hovering high above my bed. I knew it was Billy. I focused on the light, and soon I could hear his voice, which had become even more languorous than before.

Can you hear me? I know I sound farther away but if you concentrate, you'll still be able to hear me. The more you try to listen, the more you'll be able to hear.

I'm feeling quite nostalgic. You sometimes feel that after you're dead, nostalgia. But no more neuralgia, arthralgia, fibromyalgia. None of those other "algias" plague you up here in heaven. Did I say heaven? I guess I did.

I was floating all alone enjoying becoming the Universe, and what happens? Along comes Ingrid, my first wife. I cannot convey the joy, which is way too small a word to describe what I experienced when I got my first look at Ingrid in spirit form. The last time I saw her we were both on earth and she was on morphine, dying of cancer.

Ingrid was now also becoming the Universe. Her suns and moons and stars were arranged in a constellation that resembled the shape of a woman. She was doing this very feminine dance of love, moving her gorgeous starry hips back and forth as she circled around my Universe with hers. Ingrid has always been quite a seductress. Seeing her like that almost tempted me right back into a body again. Almost.

As soon as I saw this dancing Universe, I knew right away it was her. I think each soul has its own particular qualities and when you've been really close to someone, you recognize their soul no matter what form it takes.

Ingrid's soul wasn't old or young, just what you might call ageless. As she got closer, I could see that the stars in her Universe reflected different phases of Ingrid and her story. All the ages and stages of her life were there.

In one star I saw an innocent blonde baby digging up sand on a beach. In another, a scantily dressed teenage Ingrid danced on stage in Las Vegas. God, she was gorgeous. There was a star that showed her strung out on cocaine, and one of her doing time in jail. I can see that's where she got her mean streak. Then, there was my favorite Ingrid, my voluptuous Swedish bride, looking at me with those big green eyes like I was the whole world. Ingrid the crazy tigress with the hair-trigger temper was also there in the stars, but it was blended in, so it didn't seem so bad [laughs].

Shining through all these different aspects of Ingrid was her soul. And her soul was, without question, the most beautiful thing I've ever seen. I never even had a vague idea of her Divine magnificence when we were alive.

If I could have seen the ravishing beauty of Ingrid's soul while I was alive, I would have been so overwhelmed I don't think I could have functioned. But here, I'm just drifting in space, floating around, becoming the Universe. There's nothing I really have to do.

If you have things you have to do, seeing people's souls could be a big impediment. If people could see each other's souls, the whole world might shut down. Think about it. You'd go into a store to buy something and get hung up for hours marveling at the cashier's soul. If you saw the soul of your so-called enemy, you'd probably fall in love with them, and then what? And if you beheld the soul of someone you already truly loved, like I did with Ingrid, the intensity of that experience might incapacitate you for the rest of your life. You can understand why seeing souls could be a problem on earth. It would become one big love-in.

I guess because Ingrid and I are now both Universes, we're ready to gaze upon each other's souls. There's nothing we want or need from each other except to float around and enjoy the light. That's it. No words, no attachments, no demands, just two Universes passing in the light.

Are we the Universe? Google it.

Billy was speaking even more slowly than last time, and his speech was slurred. I sensed it was becoming harder for him to communicate with me.

When I searched "Are we the universe," a YouTube video of the late astronomer Carl Sagan came up. In it, he describes how we're all made of "star stuff"; how billions of years ago the elements of our bodies were formed from stars, and how our desire to explore the cosmos is really a longing to return to our celestial origins. Whoa! That's exactly what Billy was talking about. And it's not only Billy who is made of the cosmos. We are all literally made from stars. Becoming the Universe isn't just a poetic image. It's grounded in scientific fact.

FOURTEEN

I Don't Know

For the next few mornings I saw Billy's blue light as I woke up, but it vanished quickly. Finally the light lingered, and when I focused on it, I could hear Billy's voice. It was barely audible and even more distorted than before, but through intense concentration I was able to make out his words.

We haven't spoken in a while—or have we? It's not easy to speak in my new state. My thoughts have so much space between them it's an effort to string them together, but I'm doing it for you. What's a gift without a little effort? Don't be scared, honey, because of the difference in my voice. It's still me, I think. I'm laughing; can you hear it?

With all this space between my thoughts, the past has become unimportant to me. If the past was different, would it matter? Would I still be where I am now, talking to you and having the greatest experience of my life, I mean death? I don't know.

What's important now is that I have been delivered to this bliss that is beyond pleasure, beyond joy, beyond anything that can be imagined. My present bliss factor is four hundred million times the potency of the healing chamber I was in right after I died.

I have to get used to talking to you from this new stratosphere. I'll try to dial into my previous state of consciousness. Wow! From this dimension memories are psychedelic, stereo-symphonic—what's that word I'm searching for that has to do with computers?—virtual, virtually enhanced. But I can't hold onto the memories. They come and go, and there's no landing or impact. Death is really amazing.

I'm alone, but I'm everything. It's difficult to explain things when there isn't thought. There's nothing that I so-called want or need. Satisfied is much too small a word because it implies fulfillment of some lack, and lack is an earth thing. I know that at this moment you're able to feel a fraction of a fraction of my bliss, something inside you that's luminous and healing.

Remember this, my darling—remember this. What you achieve on earth is only a small part of the deal. If there's a secret I could whisper, and that you could keep, it would be that it's all inside you already. Every single thing you need. Earth is just a stopover. A kind of game. Make it a star game. If I could give you a gift, it would be to teach you how to stay free inside that game, to find the glory inside yourself, beyond the roles and the drama, so you can dance the dance of the game of life with a little more rhythm, a little more abandon, a little more shaking-those-hips.

Billy was dictating so slowly it took almost an hour for me to transcribe his words. But it didn't bother me. Nothing bothered me. I was ready to make my life a star game, whatever that was.

That evening, around seven, Billy interrupted my dinner with an unusual invitation.

Meet . . . me . . . at . . . the . . . ocean.

I put my food in the fridge, slipped on a heavy sweater, threw a blanket in my car, and drove to the ocean. The air was soft, the stars bright, a yellow crescent moon hung in the sky.

"How do I make my life a star game?"

Become . . . the . . . Universe.

I tossed my blanket aside and lay down in the sand. In the endless expanse of sky above me, stars sparkled like diamonds. Soon, Billy's presence pulled me up and up and up and whirled me around, as if I was falling up a hole instead of down. I fell upwards into the starlight, faster and faster, becoming lighter and lighter, dissolving into space. Then, my fear kicked in and landed me back in my body lying in the sand.

All the things I usually take so seriously suddenly seemed insignificant—specks against the vastness of the Universe. Billy was teaching me a star game.

FIFTEEN

New Body

I wanted to learn more about the star game, but Billy disappeared. This time I couldn't feel him around at all and the letdown was bigger than usual.

It was early July. Tex got a book deal and didn't have time for the writing group, so it broke up. People were having fun at the ocean, enjoying dinner with friends, going to parties. I was taking long beach walks at daybreak, composing spacey music on my synthesizer, and watching shows about the cosmos on cable TV. I felt displaced, outside of things. I wasn't quite grounded in my own world and didn't have access to Billy's.

Had Billy completely dissolved into the Universe? Is that what finally happens after we die? I was sad, but not the same kind of sad as I had been when I first learned of Billy's death. I loved him even more now than when he was alive. And I knew for certain he loved me back. Was our time together over?

A month after that night at the ocean, I saw the blue light above my bed. As I stared at it, excited, I heard Billy's voice, and this time it was crystal clear.

Barnabus, Barnabus, hello from Barnabus.

Hey Princess. This will surprise you. We're not only allowed to write this book—we're supposed to.

I was floating around becoming the Universe when suddenly I was sucked back into a body, a body made of light. When I was the Universe, when I was the stars and moons and galaxies, I wasn't thinking about the fact that I didn't have a body. I never seem to be doing that thing people do, thinking about what I don't have. That's because I'm so into what is. I am what is!

Instead of flesh, my new body is made of concentrated light. I'm still me, but I'm really different. Becoming the Universe has definitely changed me, prepared me for this event. I'm still ecstatic, but my consciousness is clearer and more focused than before.

So, I'm wearing holy robes and I've got a full head of curly black hair like when I was young. I also have a mustache. There's no mirror. I just know how I look. I'm still Billy, but I feel even more like myself than when I was alive. My bad-boy tendencies seem to have changed into something else. When I was alive, my so-called misbehaving was really my way of looking for my own truth down there on that very illusion-filled planet. My rebelliousness has served me well now that I'm here. Now, instead of being a wise guy, I'm a wise man.

Wisdom is coming from inside me and shining out in all directions as bliss pours from my heart. I don't have an actual heart, but it's coming from that area. I'm radiating love; I'm just pulsating with it. There's so much hate on earth, even in the name of God. What a concept!

Hate in the name of God. That's why Christ said he's the protector of the meek. They aren't such big haters.

I'm in a sky that is very, very blue. This blueness is my first experience of concentrated color on this side, and it's way beyond human imagination. On earth, your senses are separated from each other, but this blueness I can hear and smell and taste and touch.

Before, when I was the Universe, I was in a night-time sky, and my memories were see-through, like watercolor paint. I wasn't thinking about that until now that this new color thing is happening. There's that now thing again, so there's definitely some kind of time going on here. Like I had no body and now I have one. Time here has nothing to do with clocks or earth's turning. Here, time has to do with something being a certain way, and then a change. Moments are oceans ebbing and flowing and taking you with them. You're not waiting for the next one. You're just in the ride.

My new eyes are looking up at something indescribably bright, but it's definitely not the Sun. The Sun is puny compared to this giant blue-white ball of light over my head. I'll try to describe it accurately. It's a giant sphere—so big I cannot see where it begins or ends—with rays shooting out of it, and the rays are as bright as the sphere. It's the best thing I've ever seen, alive or dead. It gives me this feeling, no, this experience—it's more like you have experiences here, not feelings—that everything I ever hoped was true, is true, and is even better than I could have imagined.

So I'm standing under this blue-white sphere and a smiling radiant man comes along. I use the word *"man" to let you know he isn't some other species or anything like that. Whether he's a man or a woman doesn't seem to matter much to me. He's also wearing a robe. I'm surprised by the robe because it's brown and looks like burlap. It's the most earth-like thing I've seen so far, so I'm guessing he has something to do with what goes on down where you are. I couldn't care less about his robe, really, because the radiance of his face is so spectacular.*

I don't know him, but he seems familiar. And although I don't remember ever meeting him before, I know his name is Joseph. His hair is silver, and I think he's an elder, but he's not old. His hands reach out towards me as he looks at me with the bluest eyes I've ever seen. I know it sounds corny and contrived, but it's not. It's brilliant and oddly familiar, like I'm being welcomed home from a long journey, only the land to which I've returned, well, I've forgotten how brilliant it is. Everything is waving with energy. That's a good way to describe it. It's all energy instead of matter.

Joseph puts a book in my hands. It's not really a book, but let's call it a book for now. He just puts it in my hands and I can feel everything in it. It's such a privilege, such a gift. Gift is too small a word.

I never thought of myself as smart, Annie. In fact, some of the brilliant teachers I've had tried to convince me I was stupid. I was never stupid. I just didn't go along with the party line. They were trying to spoon-feed me their interpretation of life, instead of letting me live and find things out for myself.

Joseph looks down through a hole in a thick layer of clouds, which I now notice below us, and there you are sitting at your computer. And I know for certain that you and I are supposed to do this.

I understand. This journey we're on together can get scary for you sometimes. Having your newly dead brother appear, talk to you, show you his world, and arrange synchronicities in the form of little clues to prove to you he is real—well, it's disorienting.

Why is this happening? Because it can. Did you know that Harry Houdini spent years trying to contact other dimensions, looking for evidence of an afterlife? And even though he was the greatest magician ever, his attempts to communicate with the dead or contact the living after he died never succeeded. He was missing the essential ingredients—the right sender, the right receiver, and permission from those on this side of things.

I know you don't want people to think you're flaky. I told you before; don't worry about what others might think. That's another important secret of life. Don't live by what you "think" others think. You figured you'd maybe get around the issue by turning the book into a novel, but I'm telling you, Annie, this is better because it's real.

To be standing in the sapphire blue firmament with this book in my hands is a great honor. I always wanted to write a book. You didn't know that, did you? I wanted to share some of the wisdom I gained during my travels, help others connect to the spiritual side of life. But in my wildest fantasies, I never imagined I'd become an author posthumously [laughs].

*And don't forget to Google "Barnabus," the name I
said as you woke up this morning.*

I was stunned. For the first time, I could see
flashes of Billy's world, his shimmering robe, a flicker
of Joseph's blue eyes. And for a millisecond I saw the
blue-white sphere, which gave me a fleeting feeling
that nothing could ever go wrong again. Best of all, I
saw Billy's radiant face, with a seen-it-all, done-it-all,
bad-boy-saint knowingness in his eyes, looking up at
the sphere as if he had been expecting it to show up
all along.

I Googled "Barnabus." The first search result said:
Saint Barnabas (1st century), born Joseph

Joseph! I couldn't read another word. Being told
that we had permission to write the book, actually
seeing Billy for the first time, and this proof about St.
Barnabas being named Joseph—all of it sent my brain
into overload.

Did having permission mean I was now obligated
to tell the whole world about Billy? Was Billy trying
to persuade me by making me feel special, saying even
Houdini couldn't do what we were doing? Having
conversations with a dead person wasn't something I
wanted to be special at.

My brother wasn't the only one who could be
rebellious.

SIXTEEN

Blue-White Sphere

Iknew Billy could no longer speak to me directly. Since he started becoming the Universe, I had to focus on the blue light that appeared above my bed in the mornings, or I couldn't hear him. It was like a cosmic radio—to hear the broadcast I had to tune in. I decided to ignore the light, at least until I figured out what to do next.

For days I pretended not to see the light above my bed. Then one afternoon I walked out my front door and was shocked to see Billy above me, a pale transparent figure, floating like a cumulus cloud in the sky. He wore a white robe and was reading a large book that he held open in his hands, a book with a red leather cover just like the red notebook he had given me. Was my imagination creating cartoons, or was Billy using his new body to get my attention? And who was giving him permission to do that? Whatever it was, ignoring Billy was no longer an option. The next morning when I saw the blue light I tuned in.

Thank you for honoring me by finally sitting down at your computer to write my words. Were you surprised to see me in the sky yesterday, with the red notebook in my hands? Having my new body does give me certain advantages [laughs].

How can I describe the blue-white sphere? Picture your own sun blazing about twenty feet above your head, so big it covers the entire sky. This sphere is made of light, not fire, and instead of being yellow, its white core turns sapphire as it radiates out. It's so powerful that if you were anywhere in its vicinity, your flesh would evaporate in a nanosecond. Since my new body is made from its light, that's not a problem for me.

All beings on earth carry the light from this sphere within them. That's why spiritual philosophies say that we are one. Where I am, this isn't just a theory. I see the blue-white light everywhere, in everything—in me, as well as in you.

The light from the sphere propels your soul into your body when you're in the womb. It then becomes the invisible force that gives you life. And when the time is right, this same light launches your soul right up into the healing chamber at the moment of your so-called death.

And, just like me, one day you will get a gorgeous new body made of the light from the blue-white sphere. Then, instead of carrying the light inside you, the light will carry you inside it. That will happen when you're living where I am now, in a realm that has no shadows.

In your world, as the earth moves around the sun, there's nothing but shadow for a good part of the time. The mystery of life on earth cannot exist without the shadow element. You cannot have the sea without storms, the earth without quakes, the wind without *tornados. On earth, when the light rises, the darkness comes with it. Where there is light, there is shadow . . . unless it's midday. But it can't always be midday, Princess. And sometimes—sometimes darkness is okay too. Don't overlook the riches contained in the darkness. Life's very temporary, so don't let time just pass. Let the moments fill you—the ones you judge to be good as well as bad.*

Remember, the blue-white light is always inside you. And every day, by remembering it, you feed it, and it will grow. When life is joyous, the light will be there. When there is hardship, the light will also be there.

I know you're afraid that things will go wrong. They will. It's like that on earth. We're all permitted our pain, but pain is a transitory state. My transition was to death, to this comfort and love I now receive in every molecule of my being. Know that the shadow is illusory and temporary. Bliss, ultimately bliss and light, are the truer and stronger reality.

Who but you could I tell these secrets to, my darling? Who but you could share my journey through the worlds beyond? And who but you could help me write this book?

After transcribing the above, I was almost shaking. This time, instead of making me euphoric, the energy intensified my inner conflict. Billy, Joseph, and whoever else in their dimension gives permission for this kind of thing wanted me to do something I wasn't ready for. But if I said no to the book, would I be denying the wishes of a higher realm? Would there be consequences?

I went outside, hoping to see my brother in the sky again, but he wasn't there. This was one of the few times I would speak to Billy out loud.

"I'm sorry, Billy," I said, "but I can't do this. I don't want to write this book with you. It scares me. I don't know why, but whenever I think of your book being published I feel terrified. If people were supposed to know what happens after death, it wouldn't still be such a big mystery, would it?" I was close to tears. "I'm sorry to disappoint you, I love hearing you, I love listening to you, but I can't write this book. Please don't stop visiting me."

SEVENTEEN

Quantum

When I woke up the next morning, I studied the ceiling for even a hint of blue light, but there was none. Not that morning, or the next, or the one after that. In an effort to coax a visit from Billy, I started sitting at my computer just after dawn, looking out my glass doors and up at the sky.

A little more than a week later, Billy appeared in the sky again, this time doing an impersonation of a bad-boy angel. A sparkly toy halo, like one you'd buy at a party store, sat crooked on his head; he had an exaggerated saintly expression on his face. Every once in a while he'd look at the red notebook in his hands and make faces as if he were reading the most interesting, surprising words ever written. This was exactly the way Billy would fool around when he was alive. Even though what I was seeing made me question my sanity, I was glad he was there.

For the next few days, when I was outside, Billy the bad-boy angel would often pop up. I'd be walking in town, talking to an acquaintance, putting gas in my car—and there he'd be, hamming it up in the sky. He appeared when other people were around, but I was the only one who could see him. It was our secret.

After three or four days of this, when I woke up and saw Billy's light above my bed, I went straight to my computer and tuned in.

I know one of the reasons you're hesitant to share these writings is because you want to protect our relationship from ridicule, and I thank you for that. But darling, there isn't anything to protect really, is there? All we're doing is telling the story. Let it be up to each individual to take it or leave it. Some people will believe it's true. Others will say "perhaps," but "perhaps" is a big improvement over "no way."

Everyone on earth is eternal, but they don't know it. They may sort of believe it, but they don't know it. That's because it's too much to know. Eternity is not a concept the mind can grasp. You can try to imagine it, but then, not being able to experience it, your mind says, "Yeah, I think it's a terrific story, maybe true," but ultimately it rejects what it cannot understand. That's because it isn't your mind that can grasp all of this. It's something much bigger and more real than your mind.

Let's take you, for example. Even though you're the one having these experiences, you still don't completely accept the whole thing, do you? Why? Because your earthliness is rising up against the reality of me talking to you from a different sphere. Darling, this is more than a book. I want to help you and others expand your consciousness. Make a quantum leap.

What do I mean by that? Well, let me give you Billy's version of quantum—quantum in a few easy steps.

What's the shortest distance between two points, the quickest way to get from here to there? Is it a straight line? Not really, because you're already in both places. People say you can't be in two places at the same time, but they're wrong. Wherever you want to go, you're already there. And wherever you don't want to go [laughs], you're already there too. Quantum requires keeping your focus on where you want to go.

What's a quantum leap? It means that a change in perspective is a powerful thing. It means that the way you see something can actually change that something. The experiment you're so fond of, Schrödinger's cat, is about quantum. Basically, it postulates (you like that word?) that how you observe something changes that something.

Schrödinger's Cat—Billy's Version

Daddy didn't care for cats, wanted nothing to do with them. When Daddy looked at a cat, he saw a mean creature with long, sharp claws. You look at a cat and see heaven. Do you think that might affect the cat?

Quantum usually applies to subatomic particles, not to people. But people are actually vast universes of subatomic particles, and sometimes a shift in perspective makes the particles do a different dance, leap into a new reality. That's why I'm saying viewpoint is everything. Okay, not everything, but a lot.

I've been standing in the sky for days, impersonating an angel in order to get you to take yourself a little less seriously, sit at your computer again and write. For me, days are an eternity. Wow—eternity, Annie, think about it. Don't worry, Greta Garbo. I'm not talking about an eternal life on earth [laughs]. *This is different.*

If you want to make a quantum leap, build a bridge with me between your world and mine. Take a chance. Shift your viewpoint about writing this book and come on this journey with me. Because if you could escape the smallness of your mind and live in the dimension of my blessings, if you could dance this dance with me, you would experience something you've barely imagined, something you've dipped your toe into now and again. Instead of a toe, let's try to get you to come in up to your ankles, then your knees, then your thighs, then your waist. Little by little, let's get you to come into the ocean of your Divine Essence.

Billy was doing the same thing he did when he was alive: using his humor and charm to get what he wanted. His silly angel imitation got me thinking that maybe writing this book wasn't as serious as I was making it. Floating around the sky as a bad-boy angel was Billy's way of saying, "So what! No big deal! Don't worry about it. Come out and play."

Since Billy's death, I had become more and more isolated. I kept my answering machine on all the time and only took calls from friends who knew about Billy. When it came to everyone else, how could I act normal when I didn't *feel* normal? I found excuses not to see people. Maybe my Universe had expanded, but my physical world had definitely shrunk. I was molting inside the Billy secret.

After Billy dictated his notes, he invited me to come to the bay. Now that I could see Billy as well as hear him, it was almost as though he was a friend who lived down the street.

The day was warm, with a wild breeze. I put on a red bathing suit I hadn't worn in years and strolled down the steps to the water. Just as I reached the shore, there was Billy, unmistakable, in the sky. He was in angel mode again, luminous and white-robed, so transparent he was almost invisible, raising his hands above me, pouring down blessings. He kept repeating:

The world is your oyster
The world is your oyster
You are the pearl
And the oyster

I saw silvery sparkles everywhere. Even though I was wearing sunglasses, the light was so bright I was afraid that when the blessing was over I would discover that I had gone blind. Eyes half closed, I waded tentatively across the pebbled bottom into the calm, warm water of the bay. As I floated on my back, eyes shut tight, I whispered my new mantra, "I am the pearl and the oyster."

When I got home, I took a magazine from the mailbox and flipped open the cover. On the first page was an ad showing a blonde in a gold gown slumped against the floor of an oyster bar. The bar and floor were covered with huge piles of discarded oyster shells. The exhausted woman was staring at an object she held between her fingers. When I looked closer, I saw that it was an oversized sparkling pearl.

EIGHTEEN

Supra World

The day after I received Billy's pearl in the oyster blessing, I woke up feeling like I had a wicked hangover. When the energy from Billy's world got intense, it scared me. I wasn't afraid of the energy, exactly. I was afraid of the crash that followed after I'd traveled between his world and mine.

People who've had near-death experiences often say they didn't want to return to this world because the one beyond felt so much better. When Billy visits, I'm enveloped by a higher atmosphere. But unlike my brother, when he's finished talking, I have to come back to earth, and it isn't easy. Billy is radiating with bliss. I have a cold. He's wearing holy robes. I'm doing laundry. He's floating around becoming the Universe. I'm stuck in traffic. I'm restless. Time's passing and I still don't know what I'm doing with my life. Billy lives beyond time where moments flow into one another and he never has to think about what to do next.

Billy let me know he understood what I was going through.

Every time the presence of my world gets really strong, you get scared something bad will happen to you. Don't worry. The light from my world won't harm you, Princess.

There are many worlds, and the afterlife has many forms. Where you go, who you meet, and where you meet them is different for different people. When Daddy died, after he went through the healing chamber, he didn't find himself floating through the Universe like I did. He made an extra stop on his journey up the cosmic elevator. He landed in a place that more closely resembles people's ideas about heaven. Let's call it the Supra World.

The Supra World is a very accommodating place. Things there are designed for the comfort of the newly dead soul. One of the things people do in that world is learn to let go of certain fears—fear of death, fear of not having a body, fear of punishment. And in most cases the newly dead have a strong desire for reunion with the people they loved on earth. The Supra World is where that happens.

Daddy wasn't afraid of death but he was really looking forward to seeing his parents and his three brothers, who had all died before him. During the last months of Daddy's life, when cancer was taking him, he told you his mother and father were nearby, making his passing sweet, even though he was in a lot of pain. They were as real to him as I am to you now.

After he died, Daddy reunited with his parents and his brothers in a way he had imagined many times. When you meet your wife or husband or family or friends, or even your pets (yes, you can meet all your cats), it's more loving than it was on earth. I know this sounds idealized, and it is idealized. That's because the Supra World is built on the world of human ideas.

Do people have to wait in the Supra World until everyone who wants to see them has died before they can move on? No. It doesn't happen like that. You see, after you're dead you're able to be in more than one place at a time.

So, for example, even though I've never even been there, when Mommy dies I will meet her in the Supra World and give her all the love she always wanted from me. From my higher realm I can visit all the levels below, so the Billy suitable for the Supra World will meet Mommy there. This visiting phenomenon shouldn't be too hard for you to imagine. I'm hundreds of light years beyond where you are but I can still visit with you—right?

Aside from reunions, the Supra World is also the place where the newly dead play out strong beliefs they had about death while they were alive. It's like a spool of ribbon unwinding. The spool gets thinner as the beliefs are played out. At first, the Supra World death drama— with its angels, pearly gates, harps, and such—is very fulfilling. As a person gets more familiar with the new atmosphere, these ideas lose their grip. Beliefs are kind of like toys. As you grow up, you lose your fascination with them and they get discarded.

Beliefs are big on earth. People collect them. Some of these beliefs are helpful, but others just keep you running around trying to follow rules that others have laid down. They don't have a lot of personal meaning. It's a good idea to sort through your beliefs now and then and throw out the ones that don't serve you.

Everyone who dies eventually leaves the Supra World and goes on to watch their hologram projected onto the virtually enhanced screen of the Universe. But they won't watch it through human eyes, through the lens of good and bad, as they saw it on earth. By the time you're ready to view your life, you've left behind a lot of human concepts and you're looking through divine-colored glasses. Humans don't usually get to experience the full magnificence of their lives while they're living it. They get caught up in lots of ideas and lose sight of the miracle that is their life.

I wasn't really afraid of death, and by the time I died there was no one in particular I wanted to meet. I also didn't have a lot of beliefs left, spiritual or otherwise. Everything had been lost during my last few years on earth, except my longing for God, and the feeling that there was something big waiting for me when my life was over. I skipped the Supra World completely. It's very pleasant there really, but nowhere near as blissful as where I went. People usually need to be prepared for that kind of bliss. No one had to prepare me. I was ready for ecstasy.

Why I chose to walk my particular path on earth is beyond human understanding. Why would anyone go down that road? Well, for me, the drama of my drug addiction was one of the most interesting parts of my life. It was a very important struggle. And in my case, losing prepared me for a big win. I couldn't know it then, but my ordeal on earth was getting me ready for what was to come.

You see, after hologram review most people don't go on to becoming the Universe. But don't worry, that's fine with them. It's different here than it is on earth. No one wants to go someplace other than where they're going. Some souls go back to your planet to reincarnate and others go to places in the afterworlds to develop more and prepare for the becoming the Universe experience. You wouldn't be able to tolerate that event if you weren't ready for it.

I was an incurable drug addict who wasn't even capable of making a living. Who would have thought that I would be ready for becoming the Universe? Well, that just shows that you can never judge anyone's life, yours included.

Sometimes in hardship you're forced to stand alone, and standing alone prepares you for becoming the Universe. I'm certainly not suggesting anyone take my path. Definitely not. But I am recommending that you see through your own eyes, not through the lens of others. Make your life as interesting as you can. Take chances. Go after your dreams.

Maybe these pages will give you a sneak preview into the many worlds and endless possibilities that lie before you. Maybe you will begin to play with the idea that you are eternal, that you will go on. You may not go on in the way you imagine, but it just may be greater and more magnificent than you could ever conceive.

After the morning's dictation, I drove to the ocean. What a beautiful mid-summer morning it was—a clear blue sky, just a few puffy clouds. As I walked along the water, a gentle breeze swirled over me and I challenged Billy for the first time.

"Give me some kind of sign, right now."

At that precise moment, Mitzi, my dog from childhood, my favorite gift from my father, came running down the beach toward me, excitedly wagging her tail like an old friend. Okay, it wasn't actually Mitzi, just her exact double; same size, same honey blonde mix of fox terrier and beagle, same soulful eyes with thick white eyelashes. As I bent down to pet her, she licked my face. If her owner hadn't shown up, I would have taken her home with me.

I had my sign.

When I got home, I called the Mercedes dealer for the fourth time. He swore he'd send the things from Billy's smashed-up car right away. I wasn't holding my breath.

NINETEEN

Saga of the Pearl and the Oyster

A summer thunderstorm woke me in the middle of the night. The wind battered through the trees, the way it had for days after my brother died. Unable to fall back asleep, I was reflecting on how much I'd changed since then. Now that I believed that other dimensions existed, I'd never be able to think of life or death, myself, the cosmos, or just about anything else the way I used to.

Soon, Billy's voice came through the wind.

Hello, and I love you.

> *The world is your oyster*
> *The world is your oyster*
> *And in the oyster shell you will find*
> *Many pearls*
> *Pearls of wisdom you will cast before all*
> * creatures*
> *I will place in front of your chariot*
> *Seventeen horses of white*
> *Beautiful horses*
> *With golden raiment*

When I first said, "the world is your oyster," it sounded pretty good, right? Like all these gorgeous pearls would just be coming your way and you'd be living on so-called easy street. But the saga of the oyster and the pearl is more complicated than it first appears. The pearl only happens when sand gets inside an oyster and irritates it.

The world is my oyster? Full of irritation? What kind of blessing is that?

It's not my fault, Princess. I know. You'd like to just la-di-da through life, easy does it, instead of being stuck with a sandy oyster [laughs]. If I give you Billy's prescription for making pearls, would you like that?

Yes, I know, the irritation doesn't feel good, but without it there would be no pearl. Don't focus too much on the irritation. Try to relax about the sand. If you deal with the sand creatively, you'll have a gorgeous treasure.

To be a pearl maker, your oyster needs a good strong shell to protect you from a hundred million irritants in your environment. Your shell helps you tell one grain of sand from the other. You know which one can become a pearl and which one isn't worth the irritation.

If you become a really smart oyster, with a good shell, you can live life with more abandon because you don't have to worry so much about the sand.

"Oh, there's that sand again. This always happens when I take a big bite out of the ocean. I'll spit most of it out and won't be too concerned about the rest."

And why don't you have to be too concerned? Have you looked inside an oyster lately? It's soft, fertile, and unformed. The inside of your oyster is your creative spark, your pearl-making laboratory. Smart people work in laboratories, right? Well, since you are the Universe, your laboratory is run by none other than the Universal Intelligence.

The same Intelligence that grows trees from seeds, that lets birds fly, that waves the ocean and gives birth to new stars—that same Intelligence also breathes your breath, beats your heart, and heals your wounds.

How can I say that you are the Universe? Because I have become as small as the smallest quantum particle, and as big as the multitude of galaxies that exist in space. I was always like that, really. I just didn't know it. And so is everyone else.

Look at pictures of the Universe. Then close your eyes and imagine those stars, clouds, comets, and galaxies inside and all around you.

When you turn your attention to the limitless, the irritation seems small compared to the sun and moon and stars. When you imagine the infinite, you're touched by your infinite self.

When I opened my e-mail that morning, I had a message from Guru Guy with a link to photos from the Hubble telescope. There was the breathtaking Universe right on my screen; cat's eye nebulas, light ring galaxies, stars being born. The link showed up at just the right moment with no effort on my part.

Early the next morning I made the three-hour drive to my mother's apartment in Brooklyn, a trip I'd taken every week since my brother's death. On the way, Billy told me something good would happen. I was glad to hear that because it was heartbreaking to see my take-charge, eighty-year-old mother hanging on by a thread.

The first month after Billy died my mother cried almost every second of every day. Then the doctors started shoving all kinds of antidepressants down her throat until she was practically catatonic. She sulked around her apartment in a robe, and stopped having her hair styled, putting on makeup, or getting her nails done. She acted like an old lady, which she had never done before.

Soon, my mother was reading countless books about death. The one she was absorbed in when I arrived that day talked about people losing their souls as a punishment for being "bad."

"Where is he?" she cried in my arms. "Where's my baby boy? Has he lost his soul?"

"No, Mom, Billy's soul is fine. I wish I could find a way to help you believe that."

"I never realized how much I loved him," she said. "I always thought I loved you more, but it isn't true. I loved him just as much. Now he'll never know."

"Don't worry. You'll be seeing him soon enough. Then you can tell him whatever you want."

That made her smile.

I brushed her white hair, put cream and lipstick on her face, and helped her get dressed. "It's a lovely summer day," I said. "Let's go walk by the river." The sun was shining, bouncing off the Hudson, as we strolled arm in arm down the promenade.

"I need some wisdom, Mom. My life's still a mystery to me. You've lived a long time and learned a lot. What wise thing can you tell me?" Asking her for advice was my way of helping her remember how smart she was.

"It's funny, I knew you were going to ask me that question and I knew how I would answer. I just read a book about a Chinese mother and daughter. I think it's called *Scattered Pearls*. As the daughter was about to leave for America, the mother told her that whatever troubles life brought her she should think of them as sand in an oyster and make them into beautiful pearls. And that's what I want for you, my darling girl. Take the hard things and make them into pearls."

I laughed and said, "You won't believe this. I left something back at your apartment to show you."

Many times I'd told my mother about Billy's visits, but she didn't want to read anything he said. I'm sure she thought I was living in some kind of Billy fantasyland that made the cold hard truth of his death even more painful. I understood, but now I sensed she'd be receptive.

When we got back to the apartment, I read her Billy's notes about the pearl and the oyster. My mother scrunched up her forehead and was quiet for a minute. Then she burst out laughing.

"All this time I was just humoring you when I said I believed Billy talks to you. But now, oh my God, I have to believe it!"

My mother opened her turquoise jewel box and handed me a string of pink baby pearls. "Why wait until I'm not around anymore. Then I'll never see you wear them."

After our visit, my mother's melancholy began to lift. She confided that sometimes when she woke up she thought she felt Billy's spirit around, healing her and helping her get well.

"Even though the pain of losing Bill was like no other I felt in my life," my mother said, "God meant for me to know him and love him, I am sure of that."

TWENTY

Book of Life

O n a dreamy mid-August morning, before
dawn . . .

*It's a beautiful day. Why not bring the red notebook
and join me at the beach?*

When I got there, the sky's pink and orange streaks
gave way to Billy's ethereal white-robed glory.

*It's a good day where you are, my sister. Every day's
a good day here, although there really aren't days and
nights. But I don't miss them. I don't miss a thing.*

*One of the things I certainly don't miss is being
concerned about the way I look. Here, I just look like
myself and that's great. There are no pretensions or
efforts to appear any which way. I just radiate, which is
effortless. Since I'm made of light, I don't have organs or
blood or anything like that. No knee problems, no liver
problems, no drug problems, no weight problems. I don't
have a home either, except my light body.*

*Sometimes I leave my light body and go back to
becoming the Universe; I let go and do some more
blending into the cosmic energy field. I guess you could
say it's a bit like human sleeping because they're both
about letting go. But really there's no comparison,*

because becoming the Universe is sheer ecstasy and sleeping is hit or miss.

On earth, you need day and night, sleeping and waking, birth and death. You need to know that today may have been difficult, but tomorrow could be better. You may have messed the day up, or the day may have messed you up, but you can go to sleep and wake up, and maybe feel like you have a fresh start.

Death gives you a fresh start just like sleep does. We don't usually think of death as a start, but that's what it is. Whatever so-called mistakes you've made, it doesn't matter now, because there's always another chance, another lifetime even, to try something different. And don't worry. So-called mistakes are okay. They're just part of the deal.

After you're dead, everything is actually more alive. Take, for instance, my Book of Life, given to me by Joseph, that dazzling silver-haired man I met under the blue-white sphere. Although I'm calling it a book, it doesn't have pages and words. It's more like an oscillating rainbow. I'm calling it a book because that implies a gathering together of information. Also, Book of Life has a nice ring to it.

Before each soul comes to earth, its own personal edition of the Book of Life is written. Life on your planet is about dramas that change you. Isn't it funny that most people are scared of change, when changing is the double fudge frosting on top of the cake of life?

And although much of your life is planned out, there's a lot of freedom inside that plan. The circumstances are like lines in a kid's coloring book, but instead of ink the lines are penciled in; they're erasable. As you color in the spaces, you influence the lines.

Reading my Book of Life is different from watching my hologram. There was no analyzing going on then. Now, Joseph and I are looking at how the particular colors I chose shaped my life.

Joseph looks like a human being but he's made of light, like me. I don't think he's an embodiment of one of the Higher Beings I spoke about before. My sense is he's working under the umbrella of their benevolence. Joseph's better looking than the best-looking actor you've ever seen. His face has experience and goodness etched right into it. His attitude about everything is not at all serious; it's lighthearted and wise. I don't know if everyone here sees things the way Joseph does because I haven't come across any other locals so far. But I can tell you that Joseph's perspective is perfect for me.

Even though Joseph knows so much more than I do, he doesn't impose rules or give me opinions unless I ask. He doesn't dominate me in any way, and that's a beautiful thing. There's so much influence from others when you're on earth that in a way you don't get to live your own life. You get to live your own life after you're dead.

What exactly does Joseph do? The best thing he does is love me unconditionally. On earth people talk about unconditional love, but until you've actually been loved that way it's impossible to understand the power of it. It goes way beyond acceptance because acceptance implies that you like some parts of me and not others

117

but you accept it all. To Joseph, everything about me is extraordinary. What an experience!

I really didn't do a bad job on earth with the circumstances I chose. They weren't easy circumstances. A lot of my life was preparing me for my new job—writing this book with you. It's hard to help others if you don't understand their frustrations, their disappointments, their fears, their desires, and their greatness. You can't really put yourself in someone else's shoes unless you've stood where they're standing.

I stood in a multitude of places, played a lot of different roles in my time: the addict, the philosopher, the healer, the scoundrel, the do-gooder, the do-bad-er, and my personal favorite, the bad-boy-saint. I don't mean to imply in any way that I was a saint, just that although I did my share of unconventional things, things that were against the law even, my heart and soul were always reaching for something wonderful.

Helping others was always my favorite thing. Although I never finished high school, I was always a good talker and I was always sincere. I used those gifts in my finest hours. Remember when I ran a drug center for young teenagers? I loved those kids and they knew it.

After that, I got to live out my lawyerly ambitions in my favorite job of all time, working as a liaison in the New York City courts helping people who got arrested for drug crimes. I pleaded their cases and tried to persuade the judges to sentence them to drug centers instead of prison. Of course, that was before I went to jail myself [laughs].

I am honored that my edition of the Book of Life contains these writings I am placing in your charge. As you may have figured out, I've become sort of a helping soul again. I hope through these pages people will realize they are not alone. I hope they will feel their immortality, even for only a fraction of a second, so they can lose some of their fear of dying. Then, not only will they have a more terrific death, they will also have a better life.

And, did I mention that within these pages there's light?

Oh, and I'm sending you a star today.

Billy's radiance made me feel so peaceful I lingered on the beach without a care in my head, gazing upwards, looking for the star Billy promised. The sea, the sand, and the gulls sparkled with the subtle light of the Divine.

That afternoon, as I drove into New York City to get my hair colored, I was thinking that of all my brother's roles, Billy Fingers was my least favorite. I hated that name. It scared me. It hinted at deals gone bad, jail, guns, and turning up dead in an alley.

"What are you, Bill?" I'd ask. "A gangster? A pickpocket? A bookie?"

Many times I'd wished my brother was something else—a professor, an author, a businessman—rather than someone whose greatest pleasure was getting high on drugs. Sometimes I was even ashamed of him. Like in high school when the brother of my best friend didn't want her to be friends with the sister of the town drug addict. Never mind that I was an honor student helping her realize how brilliant she was.

As I parked my car, I was thinking that although my brother's life was different than the one I would have wished for him, I never wanted a different brother, one who wasn't Billy. I was also thinking that maybe I'd have my hair made sunnier for the sunny days of summer—put in some highlights.

That's when Billy's voice came through my windshield.

Why don't you make your hair the color of Lena Olin's, the actress?

I laughed as I walked to the salon. "What do you know about hair color, Billy?"

While I waited in the colorist's chair, a woman sat down next to me. I felt a strange, magnetic pull in her direction, so I turned my head to look. There sat the beautiful Lena Olin.

Billy had literally sent me a star.

TWENTY-ONE

Soul Tribes

Billy's talk about his many roles made me wonder about mine. Was I a cosmic detective exploring the ultimate mystery—what happens after you die? Billy wasn't just giving me information, he was giving me proof. And the plot had been set up perfectly. I'd left my life in New York City in search of a new one at a house by the bay. Without knowing it, I had set the stage for Billy's entrance. This wasn't just Billy's Book of Life, it was mine, too.

As the steamy days of August were coming to an end, Billy gave me some more secrets.

Although all beings come from the same Source, within each individual blossom, within our differences, lies the pleasure of creation. In its multitudinous glorious playfulness, the Infinite creates diversity, so there are many soul tribes. Each tribe has its special explorations to undertake on earth.

Your soul tribe isn't about country or race, religion, or family. When you meet someone from your tribe, you feel you somehow already know that person. Other tribes are unfamiliar, but they bring gifts of new knowledge and wisdom. The different tribes provide all the characters needed for the great cosmic drama.

Many elaborate symbols appear throughout my Book of Life. They are written in a language I have never learned, but seem to know intimately. My beloved Joseph and I are from the tribe Lohana, and these symbols are our tribe's wisdom formulas.

Each human being carries out Divine experiments in the conditions that earth has to offer. The holy grail of the mythological journey of human incarnation is the wisdom formulas.

Not only do I understand the meaning of my tribe's formulas, but also through them I feel the essence of the souls who created them. What's surprising is how unconventional these Lohana formulas are. They contain no fixed idea of what is virtuous. These equations go far beyond human labels of "good" and "bad" and focus instead on the quality of one's light.

They also speak to a great mystery. Why would a soul forget its high origins, clothe itself in a body, and leave the Higher Worlds for the more difficult earth?

Well, my darling, because the soul loves experience and doesn't fear suffering. The soul knows it can never be injured. This doesn't mean it isn't natural for people to prefer pleasure over pain. That's part of the plan. And until you've left your world, you'll never fully understand all the whys and wherefores.

I was never fond of pain and suffering, but my end-of-life-on-earth scenario was filled with it. You might think because I suffered so much that I failed, but that wouldn't be true. Even though my life ended like a tragic opera, that was okay, honey.

I know, Princess. You're wishing I could share the Lohana formulas with you, but I don't have permission to do that. Don't worry, Annie. A lot of their wisdom is already in this book. Besides, you have your own equations that are being written as you live. And don't worry about them, either. You don't need to figure them out. Just follow your chimera, your eternal fire, and the formulas will come of themselves.

Once I could feel the earth beneath my feet again, I Googled "Lohana." I was startled to discover that Lohana was the name of an ancient tribe that originated in India. According to legend, these noble warriors were descendants of Lord Rama, a king who lived more than five thousand years ago and is still worshiped by Hindus as one of the many incarnations of God. Was Billy a descendent of Rama?

I re-read Billy's notes, looking for an answer. It wasn't there, but something Billy said grabbed my attention.

Just follow your chimera, your eternal fire, and the formulas will come of themselves.

What was a chimera?

The first search result that came up was a three-headed, fire-breathing she-monster from Greek mythology.

I kept looking.

Soon, an article called *At the Feet of the Eternal Fire* came up. It was about the fires known as the *Chimera*, which burn on Mount Olympus in Turkey. These mysterious flames come from inside the mountain and blaze skyward through holes in the rock. The *Chimera* are considered eternal—when attempts are made to extinguish them, they re-ignite.

What was my chimera? Where had my fire gone? Writing music had always been my passion, but that wasn't going anywhere. I had to admit to my Greta Garbo self that the Billy experience had lit a spark within me. Maybe being a cosmic detective exploring the world beyond was my new chimera.

TWENTY-TWO

Patty Malone

O n an idyllic September evening, while I was taking a shower, Billy said in a wickedly scary voice, "Steve is going to be very sick." Then he laughed like Vincent Price in a horror movie.

I was confused and upset. Billy had never made this kind of prediction before, and why was he using that spooky voice? Maybe this wasn't really Billy. It didn't sound like him. Maybe it was some kind of imposter trying to scare me. But why?

It was true that Steve hadn't been feeling well lately, but a specialist had assured him it was just some sort of bug. What if the doctor had been wrong? If Steve knew what Billy had said, he would freak out. Without letting him know why, I called and gently persuaded him to see another doctor.

A few days later, Steve phoned. "The doctor said I just have an infection that's hanging on. Nothing to worry about. He gave me some more antibiotics."

Again, from far away I heard Billy's sinister laugh. This time it was louder and sounded truly evil as it echoed around my ceiling.

Trying to keep cool, I told Steve, "I want you to see someone else."

"Why?"

"I don't know. Go see Florence. I'm sure she'll fit you in this afternoon."

Florence was Steve's primary doctor. Maybe the specialists were being too specialized. Steve called me from her office.

"My EKG looks suspicious. Florence is sending me to see a cardiologist." Later that day, Steve was in the hospital having an angiogram.

I knew that an angiogram often led to other things. I threw some clothes in a suitcase and headed to the city. The following morning, when the doctors came to Steve's hospital room and told us he needed bypass surgery, my head began to spin. On top of being worried about Steve, hospitals make me shaky. When I was fifteen, I had an emergency appendectomy that I almost didn't survive, a nightmare from start to finish.

Just as I was on the verge of losing it, Billy's soothing presence came out of nowhere and snapped me out of my panic. I became very calm and focused. Looking around the hospital, I didn't like what I saw. Dirty. Disorganized. When the surgeon came by to say he'd be operating on Steve the next day, I gave him the cold shoulder. Then I made some calls and located the best heart surgeon in New York City. As Steve was being lifted into a special cardiac ambulance at midnight for a transfer, I looked up at the dark inky sky and said, "Thanks, Billy."

At the second hospital they discovered that a drug Steve was getting at the first hospital could have made him bleed to death on the operating table. His surgery was postponed until the drug cleared his system.

The open-heart surgery went well, much quicker than expected. Because we caught his medical problem in time, there was no damage to Steve's heart. Billy had scared me to make sure I would be persistent. This wasn't green tea. This was life and death.

Billy stopped talking to me for a while. He knew I needed time. This last incident shook me up. I was beyond grateful, but had a lot of questions.

Before they were born, had Steve agreed to be Billy's protector during his last years on earth?

Had Billy agreed to repay the favor after he was dead?

Did Billy need permission to tell me Steve was in trouble?

If it hadn't been for Billy's intervention, would Steve have had a heart attack?

Could Steve have died?

Had Billy changed Steve's destiny?

As a cosmic detective, I was determined to find answers. But how? Each day, as the autumn advanced, Billy hovered peacefully, invisibly, silently, at a respectful distance.

Hoping for inspiration, I waited for the full moon. Seated on my meditation cushion at midnight with the scent of jasmine candles wafting around me, I wrote my questions on a notepad. It was a relief to get them out of my head and onto paper. I closed my eyes and went to where there was no thought, no space, no time.

When I blinked my eyes open an hour later, instead of answers I scribbled down the core of my inquiry: *Can the other side intervene in our lives?*

The following evening, an indigo blue October night, Billy's light rose high above me like an angel.

Annie, Annie, wake up.

Haven't I proved to you, my sister, that I am real? And much more important than the fact that I am real is that there are other places—places other than earth—that are real, full of light and love and bliss. And maybe, just maybe some light can come from those places to make life on your planet a little better, a little kinder, a little more musical.

I have a visitor with me tonight. Can you see the aura of golden blue light in the corner of the room? He's Pat, a very strong and noble spirit.

Does he remind you of Tex? He should, because he's her older brother. As you know, Pat was killed when Tex was just a teenager, killed what you would call tragically, in a plane crash, on his way home for a Thanksgiving visit.

Well, Pat is kind of Tex's guardian now. Tex's mother and Patty Malone and all those on this side of things who love Tex would like me to send her a letter, so please write this down.

Dear Tex,

Just because you're exhausted from your mom's illness and her death, you don't have to destroy yourself. Destroying yourself with alcohol isn't the greatest way to handle hard times.

I know you like the idea of fate. Well, maybe your fate is to become bigger than your addictions. Maybe this is the defining moment of your spirit. Maybe you want to stick around awhile without your body nagging at you saying, "I'm a mess."

It was really fun for me! No teeth, bloated, hair falling out, my knees killing me, coughing up blood. Oh, you can get away with it for a certain amount of time, but then there's the piper to pay.

You're giving yourself the silent treatment, just like you want to give everyone the silent treatment when it comes to this very tender subject. So I'll give it to you tender.

You're going to have to cut this out before your body starts screaming at you for attention.

Let's just start with one tiny baby step. Start to develop an awareness of what you're doing. No judgment. No false commitments. Just start letting what you're doing enter into your consciousness.

Billy

I was able to see the blue ball of light that Billy identified as Tex's brother floating in the corner of my room. I didn't understand, though, why Billy called him Patty Malone. Tex's deceased brother was named Pat, but their family name isn't Malone.

Later that morning, I called Tex.

"Billy came to me in the middle of the night and brought your brother Pat with him."

"Really?"

"And Billy gave me a letter for you. It's from Billy and Pat and all the people on the other side who love you."

"Oh my God."

"For some reason Billy mentioned the name Patty Malone. But that's an Irish name and your family's French, right?"

"Here we are again," Tex laughed. "Billy's doing it again. Malone isn't my name but my mother was Irish—she was a Malone. And her father, who was, of course, my grandfather, his name was Patty Malone. So the letter must be from my brother Pat and also my grandfather. This is amazing! E-mail me the letter right now."

I was hesitant. Tex almost always had a drink in one hand and a cigarette in the other, but I'd never seen her drunk. I was sure that the subject of her drinking was off limits, but I forged ahead.

"Listen, Tex. I have to tell you, the letter's about your drinking."

Tex was silent. I could feel the frost from the other end of the phone.

It was definitely time to hang up; I did, however, e-mail her Billy's letter.

I hoped it wouldn't end our friendship.

TWENTY-THREE

Cosmic Sound

Finally, right before Thanksgiving, the UPS man brought me the beat-up cardboard box that contained Billy's possessions. It had been sitting in the Mercedes dealer's showroom since Billy's death ten months ago. Billy had been living out of his old Mercedes until he totaled it the week before his death. Everything he'd had in that car was now inside the 10-by-19-by-13-inch tattered cardboard box with the words "Don't touch" scrawled across it in black magic marker.

I put the box next to the fireplace, just below Billy's ashes. I wasn't ready to open it. It reminded me of the old Billy, the one who got high, who had to live out of his car, who crashed it into a tree, who could have killed someone. Still, I was curious. What was in the box that the new Billy wanted me to have?

On Thanksgiving morning . . .

Why not open the box on Christmas? It's just a month away. You'll wake up to a gorgeous snow and it will be my gift.

When I talk to you, you hear the same voice speaking in the same language you've always heard. I use my

Billy voice for your benefit, Princess. We don't use words where I am. Joseph and I use telepathy to hear each other's thoughts. They aren't thoughts, really. They are much more wonderful than thoughts. These better-than-thoughts are like symphonies so gorgeous you cannot even imagine them.

On earth, people say things for a lot of reasons. Sometimes they mean what they say, sometimes they don't. There is no pretense or falseness here. There is no competitiveness or resentment. Here, our telepathic communications fill each other with beauty.

Speaking of telepathy, I know you've sometimes wondered if there's any music here. There are so many clichés about angels singing and harps playing, and you're curious if any of these ideas are true. Well, once again I can only speak for myself. There aren't exactly any of those things where I am. Here the atmosphere is filled with a soft, ambient sound. I haven't been analyzing, just enjoying, but I'll do a little analyzing for you.

There's a constant background haze that reminds me of earth's natural sounds, like wind or rain or ocean waves. It's more musical than that though, so I'm pretty sure it's created by instruments of some kind. The sounds resemble soft dreamy-type violins and cellos, flutes and horns and harps. There's also rhythm here, but it isn't steady. It's a pulsation that's constantly changing.

Recently, I began to notice that sometimes this haze bursts into a little melody and then that melody quickly disappears. This melody phenomenon is happening more and more, and I really can't say if it's the sound that's changed, or my ability to hear it.

By the way, if you could tune in, you'd hear these cosmic sounds right where you are now, because they exist everywhere. You can't hear them with your regular ears, though—just your spiritual ones. Even if your regular ears could hear the music, they're too busy listening to a hundred million other things to listen to these sounds. Your inner spiritual ears could hear them, but they're also preoccupied listening to a hundred million different thoughts.

They say a picture is worth a thousand words, but in this case instead of a picture I offer you an iTunes file. Certain music written by the composer Sibelius gives you an idea of what the cosmic sound is like. Sibelius was definitely tuned to a higher dimension. I'm not talking about his darker pieces, but download his swan music and notice how the swells of sound break into melodies. This will give you a hint of what I hear, except what I hear is infinitely lighter and more sublime.

And sometimes, baby sister, once in a while, I hear a voice, a distant feminine voice singing in some language I've never heard and don't understand. This voice has the allure of what I imagine is a siren's song, but the voice couldn't belong to a so-called siren because they lure men to their deaths and as you know I died some time ago [laughs]. *This singing is so intoxicating that when I hear it I want more. I'm not used to wanting anything, but I promise you no one could resist longing for this voice.*

Swan music? Sibelius? I'd heard of the composer but knew nothing about his music.

I went to iTunes, typed in "Sibelius," found a piece called *The Swan of Tuonela,* and downloaded the file. Melodies flowed in and out of a soft ambient haze of sound like the celestial music Billy had described.

As it turns out, *The Swan of Tuonela* is a Finnish legend. The sacred white swan swims in the dark mystical Tuonela River that separates this world from the next. It was the same role Billy had assigned me, navigating the waters between dimensions.

I e-mailed the music to Guru Guy along with Billy's notes. He sent me back an article about Sibelius that had appeared in the *New Yorker* magazine honoring the fiftieth anniversary of the composer's death.

The article said that Sibelius believed some of his music came from a Divine source. It also revealed that Sibelius had been an alcoholic. Perhaps Sibelius' addiction had been an essential part of who he was, just like Billy. Would he have been the same genius without it? Who can say it should have been some other way—for either of them?

TWENTY-FOUR

The Billy Box

A s Billy had promised, it did snow on Christmas. I started a fire, and with it, the Billy effect brightened the room.

Merry Christmas, Annie. The key you'll find in the box is a symbol of the keys to life I help you uncover. Did I ever tell you what a lovely home you have? I didn't have a home at the end. Home, as they say, is where the heart is.

The first thing I pulled from the box was an empty dented blue canister with the word "Home" and a swan painted on it. Sibelius's Swan of Tuonela?

Next came a spyglass.

In honor of your role as the Sherlock Holmes of the world beyond, Billy joked.

The box contained framed pictures and photo albums from Billy's life, pre-Venezuela. There were also several envelopes filled with photographs of him in Margarita; Billy with different women, Billy in the water, Billy on the beach, smiling and having fun.

Things don't look like they were so bad for me, do they? I was sometimes having a pretty good time there in Margarita. Not so serious, right?

We were looking over things together, discussing them. Even though Billy was somewhere across the Universe, he was also in the room with me.

There were CDs and some books: Philip Roth's *Sabbath's Theater, The Language of the Heart* by Bill W, the founder of AA, and *Living Each Day* by Rabbi Twerski. Underneath the books were four beat-up old spiral notebooks. They were Billy's journals.

"You kept a journal? Can I read them?"

I gave them to you, didn't I?

At the bottom of the Billy Box, hiding in a corner, was a pink quartz heart, a mother-of-pearl pillbox, the key that Billy said would be there, and two Alcoholics Anonymous coins.

The gold coin was from White Deer Run. My best rehab experience. Stayed straight for eight years after that.

The other coin was silver. It had a cross on it and read, *"But for the grace of God."*

My mantra when I was alive.

As I was looking though Billy's things, Tex called.

"Annie. I think I'm going to Arizona for a month. Sometime in January."

"That's a nice long vacation."

"It's not actually a vacation. I'm playing with the idea of going to rehab."

I was surprised; Tex had never even hinted to me that she thought she had a problem. Months ago, when I'd told her what Billy's letter was about, she'd turned into an icicle. I hadn't said another word to her about it.

"What do you think, Annie? Is it a good idea?"

"A great idea."

I put the key, the heart, the pillbox, and the two AA coins in the drawer of my night table. I kept the journals in a basket by my living room couch. Like the box they came in, they reminded me of the old Billy, and I was afraid to read them. After a week, I picked a journal with a purple cover and opened it at random. It read:

"As the garden grows inside you, water the flowers and don't forget that the sand of the spiritual work is only the sand in the oyster that makes a pearl. It's the irritant that makes the pearl."

No way! How could this be? I read on.

"I thank you for this beautiful life you have given me with all the speed bumps, with all the sand. I am getting ready to write my book soon."

Sand? Irritant? Pearl? Book? This isn't possible.

Slowly, over the next month, I deciphered Billy's almost illegible handwriting. I read about his struggles, his darker moments, his aspirations, and his intimacy with God:

"I want desperately to get better, but that is actually second for me. God is first because no human alone could have gotten me out of Venezuela and helped me get well again. All of the good, all of this, was God's doing. I love you, God. Keep being there, please."

* * *

"I would like to be a guide and help others polish their mirror to reflect their lives better. Use a

137

few beautiful words that can play through their lives, hold them in God's love, and help them feel better in difficulty. I may be an addict but I am also sensitive, caring, intuitive, intelligent, and wise. Show me how to take these ideas into the world."

* * *

"This is how I will help. I will be an author and write a book. The book won't be of an intellectual nature because life and its fulfillment are spiritual. Also, I want to bring laughter into the world. In my book I will only say things to help, not to sell people something that may or may not be true. My book will get done. I will do it. It's in your hands, God. Love, Billy."

* * *

"Dear God. As time gets closer, I know it's really short. I am standing at the turning point and the only thing left is to surrender to your great wisdom and strength. I am too old to listen to anyone—oh yes—I could listen to them, but I won't because I know that the dreams and victories I have worked for in my lifetime are for the good, not the bad. The only one who gets to know about these things is you, God. And I think that must be all that matters. Love, Billy Fingers"

Going through Billy's journals put me on an emotional rollercoaster. To cheer me up, Billy played a game of cosmic hide and seek. He would contact me telepathically, without words. When my surroundings became luminous and more alive, I knew he was nearby. I also began to call on him silently to see if he would respond. He didn't always, but that was part of the game, learning to recognize when he was there and when he wasn't.

TWENTY-FIVE

Tex

One blustery afternoon in mid-January, almost a year after Billy's death, while I was getting dressed, Billy visited.

Tex will be going to rehab in a few days, and I know you've been thinking that when you say goodbye to her today you'll want to give her something meaningful.

Truth is, I had my eye on Tex from the very beginning. She's one of your favorite people, and I can understand that. Tex is a rare gem, with a magical heart. When you met her, she was caring for her sick mother. That episode went on for years. Tex was always fond of scotch, but by the time her mother died she was drinking much more than anyone realized, including herself. Then she started washing some pills down along with her scotch before she went to bed. One morning—one morning that gratefully never came—Tex might not have woken up.

It's no accident that Tex is a witness to the creation of this book and that many of the proofs involve her directly. I wanted her trust. You see, Tex began talking to me right after you first told her about my visits. She never imagined at that time what was in store for her. She never knew the special gift that was to come her way.

The letter I sent to Tex—well, she read that letter although she never said anything to you about it. You might say that her brother Pat and I did an intervention from the world beyond. We kept whispering in her ear, pushing her to her strength, pushing her to take the cotton out of her ears and the blinders off her eyes. Tex is really great at saving others but not so good at saving herself.

I think it's time to give Tex the coin I promised her, don't you? That would be the AA coin from White Deer Run that arrived in the Billy Box. It is now sitting in your drawer. You can also give her one of the pictures of me that came along with it.

Almost a year ago, before the arrival of that coin in the Billy Box, before Tex admitted she had a problem, way back then, I told you I wanted to give Tex a coin and, lo and behold, the right coin has appeared at just the right moment.

Will the influence from beyond and the coin change her life?

Only Tex can answer that question.

Tex and I met at Starbucks for a goodbye cup of coffee.

"Billy finally told me which coin to give you," I said. I put the White Deer Run coin in front of her on the table.

Tex picked it up and examined it.

"It's a twelve step coin from AA," I said. "I found it when I opened the Billy Box. He didn't tell me it was for you until an hour ago."

Tex looked shocked. It was hard for her to speak. The coin made Tex's going to rehab seem fated, and Billy was part of that fate. When I gave her Billy's picture, she said, "I think I'm going to need him."

These days, Tex still smokes, still drinks black coffee, but she never has a drink in her hand.

TWENTY-SIX

The Grace Coin

After giving Tex her coin, I woke up thinking about the words on the second coin I found in the Billy Box: "*There but for the grace of God . . . go I.*" If Tex's coin was important, I figured the other one must be too.

I knew that phrase was supposed to express compassion. But didn't it also imply "Gee, I'm sorry that's happening to you, but I'm glad it isn't happening to me?" How's the person I'm saying that about supposed to feel? Does it mean that God loves me more? What kind of message was that for Billy to leave me?

As I lay in bed philosophizing about the meaning of the phrase, Billy told me to look at the actual coin. I hadn't taken it out of my drawer since I first put it there.

The words written on the coin were not what I had remembered. What was written was simply, *But for the Grace of God.*

Words are words, and wisdom is beyond words, but people need words for their minds to hold onto and point the way beyond the words.

Lo and behold, what is actually written on the coin? Simply, "But for the grace of God." That's it, the whole thing. Leaving out three little words gives a completely different meaning. The saying you thought you remembered seeing, with the extra words added in, is a compelling but slightly troubling message.

The message on the coin I left you, I'll call it the grace coin, is something else completely. The grace factor itself, the situation of how much more difficult life could be, but for grace, is a whole other matter. The coin is to give you an awareness of the grace factor.

But for the Grace of God . . . what would I have, or feel, or do, or be?

But for the grace of God . . . how much could befall us each and every moment of our lives?

But for the grace of God . . . I would never be talking to you right now, Annie. I never would be able to say thanks—thanks for loving me so much.

And why is it that some people seem to have more grace than others? Oops, you thought we could just skip over that very tough question.

Here's another secret for you, my sister. You can never measure someone else's state of grace. You can try to put yourself in their shoes but it will never be the real thing, the true thing, the soul thing. The only life you can experience intimately is your own. Everything else is just hearsay. Never assume that anyone is fortunate or unfortunate because of the way things appear to be. Fortune or misfortune is just a human way of measuring. I can attest to that.

People usually don't experience grace unless it hits them over the head with some big miracle. They aren't in tune with the constant little miracles weaving in and out of their lives every day; miracles like breathing and seeing and hearing and walking and talking and thinking and being able to feel. That's why so many spiritual paths promote the concept of gratitude. It helps you notice the grace in your life.

I always found the act of saying "thank you" more useful than trying to be grateful. It's a lot easier to say a couple of words than to try and force yourself to feel something you may not be feeling.

"Thank you" is a high message, possibly the most healing message of all. "Thank you" aligns you with the grace that comes from the Universe of soul.

That evening, I was meeting my friend and music producer for dinner in the city. While I was in the taxi, Billy told me to expect some proof during the meal.

During the main course, Billy whispered in my ear, *Here it comes.* My friend then mentioned that on his way to the restaurant he gave money to a homeless man sitting on the sidewalk. He added: "There but for the grace of God."

TWENTY-SEVEN

Stream of Life

The silver grace coin was grimy and beat up. As I washed and polished it, I remembered how when I was six years old my father had given me a silver dollar every Friday night. I'd kept these treasures in a sparkly silver shoebox with a slit my father cut into the top. I was saving for a trip to Paris. When I was up to my one-hundred-twenty-ninth silver dollar, they all disappeared, along with Billy. I cried in my daddy's arms over lost coins, lost Paris, lost brother. The grace coin made me feel like Billy was returning my silver dollars in the form of blessings.

Still, when the one-year anniversary of Billy's death arrived, I was surprised how sad I felt. Billy, however, was having a party.

I've finished reviewing my Book of Life and I'm on to a new phase. I'm using the word "finished" for your sake. It's not really like that here. Here, each moment flows into the next so you wind up with that "eternity" feeling.

As usual, I awoke from the pleasurable pastime of becoming the Universe to find myself back in my light body once again. By the way, I never confuse my body with my "self"' the way people on earth do. I'm guessing this has something to do with how effortlessly I slip in and out of it.

Anyway, when I woke up, I was sitting cross-legged next to a magical stream. This stream is so long it seems to go on forever. But because it's not very wide, maybe a few yards across, it was easy to see my dear Joseph sitting on the other side.

This is not a stream in the usual sense of the word. It has nothing whatever to do with water. It's the flow I'm referring to here. This stream is made of rippling waves of brilliant lights: violet, red, yellow, orange, green, and blue. These colors really stand out because this stream is the only thing in this location, and all around the atmosphere is pitch black.

The thing about this stream is, it moves with a flow of enchanted sound. If I had to make a comparison, I'd say it sounds like electric chimes mixed with the fading ring of a low-pitched gong. This description, however, leaves out the most critical part, the most important feature of this stream: its mystical effect.

If you could hear the stream, my darling sister, even just for a second, you would probably never feel afraid or angry, or ever be upset again. Maybe that's why you can't hear it. The earth experience is meant to feature all kinds of emotions, and that's okay. That's as it should be.

As I sat near the stream, I had no idea what was going to happen or what I was supposed to do. Again, Joseph didn't direct me, and that's great! I never liked people telling me what to do, especially since a lot of times they told me that what I was doing was wrong. By the way, you can't do anything wrong here. There is no such thing. Joseph is my guide, not my judge.

At first, I sat there watching the vibrant colors wave up and down. Before long, though, I had to close my eyes, being overcome by the stream's supernatural sound. It drew me in deeper until nothing existed except that sound. Then, something happened that I will humbly attempt to convey.

As the sound of the stream intensified, I became more and more intoxicated. Understand, in this dimension, my moment-to-moment feeling is already better than anything you can imagine. The Stream of Life was upping my natural ecstasy factor.

Soon, my me-ness started dissolving. Like the stream, I myself became ripples of chiming rainbow colors flowing into eternity. To use an expression from my day, it was very psychedelic. Then, coming from some as-yet-unknown vicinity inside myself, I began to hear this unbelievably stunning music. At first, I heard just a few notes at a time. These were no ordinary notes, though. They had the sweetness of what you would imagine angel voices to be, but they weren't voices. The tones were long and slow and blended into each other. Then the notes began stringing themselves together into these melodies, sacred melodies that had always been there, a secret my soul kept hidden from me up until that time.

Then, completely unexpectedly, the experience became sensuous. I felt physical in a way I hadn't felt since my earth life. I again enjoyed that special kind of pleasure, *the intimacy, the warmth of having a body, the body that was mine when I lived on earth. But if I took the absolute best feeling of being alive and multiplied it by infinity, as I sat by the Stream of Life I felt even better.*

This sensuality didn't make me miss being alive, though. Not at all. The mystery of life in the flesh, the particular satisfaction the soul enjoys when it's embodied, was being revealed. It's just for the delight, the delight of the differences, the different kinds of pleasures and even the pain.

What is this Stream? I'm not sure. Maybe it's the breath of the Supreme Source. I can't really say. But what I will say, little darling, is that at some moment in the great ocean of being-ness, your own soul will sit in the presence of the Stream of Life and become one with it. And as you hear your own melodies, the ecstatic mystery that is life will also be revealed to you.

Although I didn't hear any melodies while Billy was talking about the Stream of Life, my breath became sweet as honeysuckle and waves of pleasure moved through my spine. Savoring these sensations, but aware that they wouldn't last, I asked Billy for the secret to happiness.

Like the Stream of Life increased my intoxication, pleasure can increase your joy. People spend lots of time on things that make them unhappy—too much focus on the sand in the oyster. To cultivate joy, pay attention to what you like.

TWENTY-EIGHT

Sacred Scripture

I began trying out Billy's recipe for happiness. The things I liked weren't necessarily big things. I lingered over my morning cup of oolong tea, enjoying its warmth in my hand. I bought a bouquet of calla lilies when I passed a flower shop, played John Coltrane while making lunch, sang to myself while standing on line in a store, focused on what I liked most about people's faces.

Paying attention to what I liked became a spiritual practice. The salty wind against my skin. The voices of seagulls. The taste of chocolate, French perfume, scarlet anemones, the purring of my cats. I became happier pretty quickly. My world was filled with things that gave me pleasure; I just hadn't been paying attention.

Soon, Billy had more to say about pleasure.

I am now receiving the greatest gift of my journey so far. I am receiving my Sacred Scripture. This scripture has nothing to do with the kinds of lessons people on earth think they're learning. It's not about who did what to who, or if you were "bad" or "good." In fact, it has nothing to do with your actions at all.

This scripture lets me reap the rewards of my life. We all receive rewards from the life we lived. No matter how it seems on the surface, every single life is valuable in ways you cannot imagine or figure out while you're alive. Every single life is a gift. Notice I don't say "opportunity" because that means you can fail or succeed. Beyond the concept of failure or success, there's vibration.

Vibration can't be told in words. It's the language of music. Scientists exploring string theory are on to something. The Sacred Scripture of one's life is a symphonic streaming from the unseen light of the paradisiacal Source, if you get my drift [laughs].

Each person is an instrument of the Divine, composing cosmic symphonies while on earth. Some of the music is melodic, some discordant, some bright and upbeat, some slow and melancholy. No matter. Each piece will be part of your own serenade in the afterlife. All your efforts, your ups and downs, will be a mystical tune you didn't realize you were humming. Maybe, sharing what happens to me here in this world will help you feel your music.

I meet Joseph inside a multi-colored dust cloud where stars are born. Astronomers studying the skies would never guess they're looking at places they will inhabit one day. They're not going to need telescopes or spacecraft or instruments, though. It will just happen naturally.

Joseph and I float side by side through the stardust, as waves of colored lights descend from above. And, Annie, there's no way to accurately express what happens next, but I will try.

154

As the lights touch me, they transform to melodies. These melodies are evocative; they bring something out from deep inside me. They bring out memories. Not earth-type memories. The music awakens a new kind of memory. The noise and static of the world are gone, and I remember only the soul of what took place while I was alive. I live inside the innocence and awe at the heart of life itself.

The everyday has become the miraculous; the ordinary, extraordinary. For example, waking up. I experience all the changes that take place in me as I shift from dream world to waking life. I don't think I ever really felt the grandeur of waking up or falling asleep or taking a breath or laughing, crying, singing, dancing, or making love.

These memories carry the fleeting glory, the sweet nectar that is now the Divine's gift to my soul. They explode in me with the purposeless purpose of creation, the longing of the invisible to become the fruit and the nectar. Inside this music I become the essence at the heart of bliss.

In my own state of earthly bliss, I just about made it to the mailbox. Inside was an envelope I'd been waiting for. After more than a year, the insurance company of the driver who hit Billy sent me ten thousand dollars for the accident that ended my brother's life. After settling his debts, I'd have a few thousand dollars left over. I thought I'd buy myself a ring to remind me of Billy. Billy, however, had other plans. When I took the check out of the envelope, he whispered, *Go to Jamaica.*

Billy once lived in Jamaica and loved it there. As I contemplated feeling the sunshine and bathing in the warm blue water, an idea came to me. I could take Billy's ashes to Jamaica and scatter them at his favorite place in the world, Dunn's River Falls. Scattering his remains in the warm waters of the falls, where people enjoy themselves every day, seemed perfect, except for one detail.

Fifteen years ago, the only time I'd visited Jamaica, I'd gone to Dunn's River. It was a horrible trip. After a harrowing boat ride that included a conked-out motor and fear of being lost at sea, I arrived at the falls frazzled and exhausted, so shaky I could barely stand.

I had expected a gentle cascade falling into a limpid pool, surrounded by brilliant jungle flowers. Instead, I found myself at the bottom of a six-hundred-foot monster waterfall that smashed over steep, jagged, slippery rocks. I'm not particularly athletic, and climbing up those craggy rocks while water gushed over them seemed insane. I walked up the long wood and dirt staircase that ran alongside the waterfall, and as soon as I reached the top, I caught a cab back to the hotel.

The prospect of climbing the waterfall to give Billy a proper funeral was another matter altogether. No obstacle was too big to overcome. I would ascend the waterfall in his honor, and scatter his ashes on the way up.

TWENTY-NINE

The Funeral

In March, I left the icy gray world of eastern Long Island and flew to Jamaica. As soon as I arrived at the airport in Montego Bay, the Billy effect kicked in. Billy and I were different when it came to traveling. He was outgoing and warm; I kept to myself. But this trip was different; as soon as my foot touched Jamaican soil, everyone seemed to love me and the feeling was mutual.

I unpacked and put the red silk purse that still held Billy's ashes in a tray on my hotel dresser. On the fourth morning of my trip, Billy woke me up.

Today is a good day for a funeral. I bless you as you do me. Your act of scattering my remains in Dunn's River Falls will bring me your love, especially since your last visit there didn't turn out so well [laughs].

And even though you know how hard it will be, maybe impossible even, you're determined to put my ashes into those waters. I want you to know that when you put my remains into the waterfall, I will feel it, Annie. I will feel the love behind the gesture.

I know how much you want to do this, but I want you to know it's all right if you don't climb the falls. I repeat. Climbing the falls isn't necessary. No pressure. Okay?

Today, during my funeral, there will be a sign. And after the funeral, you will receive a blessing. Enough said.

Billy had left me in a playful mood. For the first time ever I asked him for something specific. I was planning to hire a private guide to take me up the falls.

"Can you do something special with my guide? Maybe his name could be William in your honor."

Billy said nothing. Then I asked him if I should leave my silver beaded bracelet at the hotel so I wouldn't lose it. I treasured that bracelet; it had belonged to my meditation teacher. I never took that bracelet off my wrist.

If the falls takes your bracelet, it will be a good thing, is all Billy said.

I put the red silk purse in a small backpack and took a taxi to Dunn's River. The first thing I saw when I got there was a banyan tree about six stories high. Tex had written a story about a banyan tree, and I really wanted to see one some day.

"This must be the sign Billy was talking about," I thought.

I rented special rubber climbing shoes, then followed the arrows to the hut where the private guides hung out. About a dozen men in red tee shirts sat around, eating, smoking, playing cards, waiting for jobs. One guide was sitting alone in the corner, staring into the distance, looking downhearted. The woman in charge turned to him and said something I couldn't hear. The guide looked at her, shook his head, and turned away. In the brief glance I got of his face, something about him reminded me of Billy.

"Excuse me. Could you come here, please?"

The man came over, reluctantly. His name was printed in black letters on the front of his tee shirt. The name Willie was really close to "William." And even though it was obvious that the guide wanted to be left alone, I said, "Willie, you're the one. I know it."

I took him aside. "My brother died about a year ago and I'm giving him a funeral today. He loved Jamaica and he loved this waterfall. I want to put his ashes into the water and then climb the falls to honor him."

That got his attention.

"I'm terrible at these kinds of things, probably the worst climber you've ever had. I'm scared I'll slip and kill myself. I need someone special to help me."

A change came over Willie. "Don't worry, honey. I'll help you," he said.

The climb is always made from the bottom of the falls to the top, so we took the stairs to the beach where the gigantic waterfall plunges into the Caribbean. I stared up at the water thundering over the steep rocks and said to Willie, "There's no way I can do this."

Willie took my hand and started pulling me into the crashing water. He was going way too fast. He reminded me of Billy, all right—Billy and his reckless ways. I broke away from Willie's grip, and as he began climbing the waterfall, I walked up the steps alongside it, watching.

When Willie got to the place where the falls formed its first pool, he stopped and waded in the water towards me. "Come on in, honey. Come on. Let's put the ashes here."

I was terrified, but I took Willie's hand, drew on all my love for Billy, and waded into the pool. I pulled the ashes from my backpack and scattered them into the water my brother loved so much. I felt Billy in the sunshine beaming down. I cried. . .and smiled. . .and cried some more. Willie also shed a tear or two. Then Willie carried me to a rock where we both sat and let the water rush over us. I felt cleansed. I'd finally given Billy the funeral he wanted.

Willie took my hand, but this time it wasn't the hand of wild careless Billy; it was the hand of Billy the nature boy, who was sure-footed and steady, could jump from rock to rock with ease, and help you make the climb.

"If I climb, I'm going to slip, Willie," I said. "I'll break my leg, or worse. I'll crack my head open."

Willie said, "I won't let you fall, honey. I promise."

"I can't. I just can't do it."

"You can," he kept saying. "You can."

I started climbing. I was scared to death. But little by little, with Willie's help I gained confidence. Where the rocks were especially slippery and steep, I held on to Willie so tightly he almost couldn't move. I was crying and thanking him the whole way up. After more than an hour, we reached the last pool at the top and leaned back into the rocks.

"This is a very spiritual waterfall," I told Willie. "And this was a very spiritual climb."

"Yes, honey, very spiritual."

When our adventure was over, Willie's sad face was now smiling. We embraced like old friends and I went to retrieve my shoes.

It was getting late and only the two women who worked at the shoe rental shop were still there. I couldn't contain my excitement. I told them about Billy, about how much he loved Jamaica, how he had lived there once, and how Dunn's River Falls was his favorite place on earth. I told them he had died in an accident a little more than a year ago, and that today I put his ashes in the falls. I told them Willie was the best guide in the world. I couldn't have made the climb without him.

They were silent. Then one of the women said, "Willie had a brother. He died about the same time as yours."

"How?" I asked.

She hesitated. "He died in the waterfall."

I changed my shoes and ran to find Willie.

"Oh my God, Willie. I just heard about your brother! Why didn't you tell me? What happened?"

"I didn't want to spoil it for you, honey. It was my day off and my family was having a picnic here. My younger brother, he had been drinking way too much. I was talking with my wife and all of sudden she has this upset look on her face. I turned around and saw my brother out there on the rocks, dancing and fooling around, acting crazy. He had no business going into the falls drunk like that! The next thing I knew he slipped and hit his head. It happened near the bottom pool where we put the ashes."

So this day had been a double funeral of sorts. How intense it must have been for Willie to hear me pleading with him not to let me slip.

"I saw it all. I watched him die. It still hurts so much," Willie said.

I took the silver bracelet from my wrist and put it on Willie's. Then I led him to the banyan tree. We sat under it, as I held his hand and told him my story about Billy and how he'd been talking to me since he'd died.

"Thank you, honey. Thank you so much," Willie said. "For the last couple of years I feel like death's been chasing me. My sister died a little while before my brother, and my father just died last week. But today was some kind of miracle. Thank you and thank your brother for me."

Willie and I held hands as we walked through the trees and flowers. He looked about ten years younger than when we met. A flute player and a guitarist appeared out of nowhere and followed behind us. We were half dancing down the path like children.

"Goodbye, honey," he said. "I'll never forget you, or Billy."

I took a long last look at Willie, memorizing his face, put a wad of money in his hand, and got in a taxi.

When I returned to my hotel, I walked to the beach. The sea was strewn with tiny purple and white flowers for as far as I could see. There were no flowers on the sand, only in the water. There was no reasonable explanation for this phenomenon. As I swam through the petals, I felt I was floating through blessings from another realm. I kept seeing Willie's happy face and knew for certain my experiences with Billy were meant to be shared.

Part Three

From Soul to Spirit

THIRTY

The Death of Memories

After I returned to New York, Billy told me to phone his ex-wife and tell her about my trip to Jamaica. I was reluctant, but Billy insisted. He said she had something for me.

I made the call. The conversation was pleasant. A few days later, a photo came in the mail. It was of Billy, smiling, standing in the rushing waters of Dunn's River Falls.

I framed the photo and put it next to my computer so I wouldn't forget what had happened at the waterfall. Willie's transformation was too perfect, too inspiring to be chance. The events at Dunn's River changed my desire to keep the Billy experience quiet.

Billy was gone for quite a while. By now, I was used to his comings and goings and looked forward to whatever was next on his agenda. On a slate-gray May morning, along with the patter of rain. . .

I'm still here, still talking to you from an unknowable, unutterable distance. I'm still here even though right after my funeral in Jamaica, I had another funeral of sorts. I went through the death of my memories.

On earth we treasure our memories, and that's okay. That's as it should be. But you have to understand, where I am there's no desire to hold on to anything, to cling to the past. Strange, how Joseph and I reviewed the life I lived with so much devotion, simply to let go of it in the end. I guess I was loosening up my memories. Now, I'm still me, minus my experience. And I can say with some authority that it's delightfully liberating.

When I say my memories are gone, I don't mean I don't remember things about earth; I do. But what happened to me there, my ties to that particular life, have now been untied—except, that is, for you, my sister. And that is a very big and unusual "except"—as in an exception is being made for the sake of the book.

How did my memories die? I was floating around in the stardust waiting for my Sacred Scripture to take me into my next memory when pure white light came down from above me. Usually, the light was multicolored. Also, Joseph didn't show up for the lightshow as he usually did. These were clues that something different was afoot.

As the white light touched me, it became a very specific memory: the memory of thousands of tiny white lights moving in and out of my worn out sixty-two-year-old body, loosening my soul from my physical self. I'd seen these lights before. In my birth memory, these same kinds of lights bound my soul to my baby body. I think my death was a whole lot easier on them [laughs].

In the heart of my death memory, I saw myself running with my arms stretched upwards, my eyes looking towards the night sky, saying a prayer as I ran toward the speeding *car. As the car hit, I felt an enormous release as I went through another kind of death. My Sacred Scripture had played itself out and all my memories exploded like a supernova.*

The explosion of my memories rocketed me through space. I moved through a starless sky past huge forms that seemed like Beings of some kind. I sped by them so fast I can't say what they were for sure. And that gorgeous feminine voice I told you about guided me like radar through the darkness, pulling me away from my past.

Leaving behind my memories is a far distance to travel. The loss of experience, the places, the people—this is what we fear about death. But don't worry. You're more than ready for it when it comes. If you were in a fragrant garden filled with all kinds of luscious flowers and plants, and in your hand was a crinkled black-and-white photo of someplace you vaguely remember, would it bother you if you lost that photo? Whatever memories I had, even the best, can't compare with getting closer to the Source. And that's what's happening. My journey is bringing me closer to the Divine Presence.

Way off in the distance, I see a radiating disc of light. This is a light I have not seen before. The Divine Presence seems to have gathered itself up into a concentrated pure white light. As I move towards this light, it calls me—not the me I was on earth. It calls me by my soul name, the soul I was before I left the Higher Worlds to go to earth.

For the first time, Billy's voice didn't come from the right. It came from directly above me and entered the top of my head through what felt like a funnel. Violet light beamed through this funnel and lit up a small area inside my brain, making me feel hyper-awake.

I was aware of the ancient Indian system of chakras, or energy centers in the body, but had never looked into them much. Now, I went on the Internet and searched "crown chakra." It turned out that one of the physical counterparts of this chakra is the pituitary, the miraculous master gland in the brain that regulates many other glands in the body. Maybe the tweak of my pituitary was why I felt so invigorated.

"Crown chakra" also brought up these results: violet light, communication with the soul, Divine inspiration, gateway to the highest spiritual influences. Maybe as Billy headed further away, he would be communicating with me through this chakra.

I began to wonder, though. As he left his memories further behind, would he still remember me?

THIRTY-ONE

Shvara Lohana

As my crown chakra began to blossom, I felt myself moving along with Billy towards the light. I started falling in love with everything—and the sun, the sky, the sea, the trees, the flowers, the birds, the butterflies, and the ground beneath my feet, all seemed to love me back. When I went into town, people who were strangers seemed like friends. Even if they weren't able to see the light, I knew they still were moving towards it. The pure joy of the Divine Presence was their destiny.

As the mid-May sun rose like a topaz in the sky. . .

Good morning, my sister. Here I am again, your on-the-scene reporter, coming to you from a new dimension.

For the first time since I died, I'm standing on solid ground, but the ground here is like nothing I've ever seen. It's luminous and kind of rough, like uncut diamonds. Think of pictures of the moon's surface. Where I am, the landscape is also bare and rocky, with craters and hills, but instead of dusty, it's glistening and translucent. Everything in this jeweled world looks like it's made of crystallized light, even the pink sky.

Now, at this very moment, as I'm speaking to you, that haunting voice is getting louder and louder and a pink mist is moving in. The mist is so fragrant, if I were able to swoon, that's what I would be doing.

Suddenly, all at once, I'm in front of the most beautiful woman I've ever seen. Beautiful is so inadequate. She must be a different species or a Higher Being. She's twice my height and very slender. Her face is gorgeous! It's like a golden pearl with exotic features. She reminds me of the goddesses they worship in India.

Her feet are adorned with rings and bracelets, and they don't touch the ground. Her dress of brilliant blue sapphires trimmed with rubies swirls out behind her. She has thick black hair down to her waist, and golden light encircles her head like a tiara. Have you seen the moon when it's golden? That's the only thing on earth that even vaguely describes her luminescence. As she floats in the air, her hands move in some kind of mystical dance.

Oh, Annie. I've never been in love like this!

And I feel very humble. I was kind of cocky about being dead, but if this would have happened right away . . .well, I wasn't ready for it. I had to be prepared for this kind of majesty.

As I stand before my Goddess, my appearance is changing. I'm getting taller and thinner, and overall I'm looking more like her. I call her my Goddess because somehow she is mine.

For the first time, my Goddess moves her perfect ruby lips. Hers is the intoxicating flute-like voice

I've been hearing all along. She sings me her name:
Shvara. It fills me like a mysterious perfume I have
been forever seeking.

Shvara smiles a smile so gorgeous and powerful, if
there could be a smile like that on earth, all war would
end and everyone would stop what they're doing and go
feed the hungry children. It is that powerfully good. I'm
not sure I could have withstood the power of that smile
before this moment.

Then, my Goddess sings me her full name: Shvara
Lohana.

Do I really belong to the same tribe as this magnificent
Goddess? I try to control myself but have to ask, "Does
that mean I will be with you forever?"

Her smile dazzles me. "In this dimension, forever is
longer than you can imagine."

I admit that sounded disappointing, but she didn't
exactly say no, right?

This time, hearing Billy through my crown chakra
opened its petals into a lush flower. As Shvara's beauty
entered my soul, my heart beat so fast I thought it
might burst. Instead, it melted like a burning candle,
filling me with molten grace.

I searched the Internet to see if the name Shvara
had any meaning. I was fascinated to learn that Shvara
is the short form of *I-shvara*, a Sanskrit word, Sanskrit
being the sacred language of ancient India. So Billy's
description of Shvara as an Indian goddess wasn't a
coincidence.

What delighted me the most, though, was discovering that in Hindu tradition Shvara means Supreme Lord. And when Shvara takes on a feminine form, she is no less than the Supreme Goddess, the one and only Goddess above all others.

Was Shvara Lohana an actual Divine Being or a vision Billy was having? Was she his personal God or was she God? Is God actually a goddess?

THIRTY-TWO

Parade of Souls

The very next morning, as the songbirds chatted away and the spring air filled with sweetness. . .

Shvara Lohana turns and a building surrounded by haze appears where she is looking. Did she create it with her gaze? I don't think it was there before. I'm excited because I haven't seen any buildings at all since I died. As the haziness clears, I can see that the building is pearly white and has huge columns in the style of Greek or Roman architecture. It's so enormous it seems to have no beginning or end, and it isn't solid. It ripples. A bridge is forming from where we are up to the White Building, so I guess that's where we're headed.

All this is wondrous, so very wondrous, and it's even more so because I'm completely and utterly in love. I can't be sure, because my memories are gone, but I think I loved a lot of women in my time. I am sure, though, that what I'm feeling for Shvara is something else altogether. I think it's called Divine love. If I were here with Jesus or Buddha or any other Supreme Being, I probably would be feeling a lot of love for them too, but whoever picked Shvara Lohana sure made it easy.

Making exotic dance movements with her hands, my Goddess floats up the bridge. I follow her with complete devotion. As she glides ahead, her unimaginably graceful feet captivate me. I could spend an eternity just looking at them. They're not just beautiful; they're benevolent and intelligent, just like the rest of her.

Shvara looks back at me, smiling. I'm so glad to be here, to rest from the work done on earth, and follow my Goddess towards the White Building. As we get closer, I see there are an endless number of bridges that lead up to it. And for the first time since I've been on this side of things, I see people, like me. Each one is walking up his or her own bridge towards the White Building. We aren't really people anymore, we're souls. Each soul resembles its floating Tribe Leader.

As the souls cross their bridges, we give each other a nod in passing, but if they're feeling anything like I am, all their attention is on their Leader. I'm trying to notice what I can for you. It's very unusual that I'm able to report these events, so treat this information as sacred. Whether or not we can put this in our book, I will let you know.

The Tribe Leaders are Beings that don't exist on earth, and each one of them is extraordinary. They all have the same golden light around their heads. Some are great warriors with shields and swords and super-powerful bodies. Some Leaders look kind of plain and humble except for their enormous jewel-colored auras that are more than ten times bigger than they are. Some look scholarly and carry parchment scrolls that unravel and trail behind them. One Tribe Leader has fluorescent orange hair and is riding a gigantic red lion, or maybe he is part lion. I can't tell. Another Leader seems to be a mix of man, dolphin, and sun.

There are Tribe Leaders who I'd describe as gorgeous goddesses, like Shvara. I'm so lucky my Leader is who she is. But I'm guessing everyone feels lucky, like they have the right one.

There's a rhythm and a sense of wild celebration to this spectacle. It's as if we were all meant to be here at this time and have been rehearsing our parts for all eternity.

Shvara Lohana has been humming softly as we ascend my bridge. I am in love with her like I've never been in love. I wish you could hear my Goddess singing:

We are the dream of the Universe
We are the whim of the Infinite
The breath and the breather
The enemy and the friend
If this is illusion
I'll bow to it
Ava lo ke tash shvara
Ava lo Tara
Ava lo ke tash shvara
Ava lo Tara

Shvara's song fills me with what I will so inadequately call compassion. I feel such tenderness for the parade of souls walking toward the White Building. Each had their own story, their own struggles, their own pathway that led them here.

How noble is the journey of each human being, from Divine to dust and back again. How brave to enter a body and dance the dance of existence only to lose everything imagined to be true in the moment of death.

As we approach the top of the bridge, my consciousness is crystal clear. I am ready, but I do not know for what.

When Billy started softly chanting the words to Shvara Lohana's song, I was spellbound. I thought he was speaking some kind of celestial language and would tell me the meaning later. But when the song was over, he asked me to do another Internet search.

The lyrics I hadn't understood were, again, actual Sanskrit words. This time they were the names of Bodhisattvas, Enlightened Beings whose mission is to assist humanity. Avalokiteshvara is the Bodhisattva of compassion and Tara is his consort. Tara sprang from a tear that fell from the eye of Avalokiteshvara as he wept for the suffering of humanity. After Billy heard Shvara's song, he also seemed to be sharing in the compassion of Avalokiteshvara.

When I told Guru Guy about these names, he told me more about the hand-painted scroll he had brought me from Tibet. It had been hanging on the wall beside my bed for the last three years. The pearlescent, four-armed, lotus-postured, golden-crowned figure enthroned in a rainbow of pink lotus flowers was, in fact, Avalokiteshvara.

"But you told me it was Chenrezig," I said.

"Chenrezig is the Tibetan name for Avalokiteshvara."

THIRTY-THREE

The Archway

June was exploding with color when the window to my brother's world opened once again.

When Shvara and I reach the top of the bridge, I no longer see the others; they have gone a different way. We are standing in front of an archway built into the stone wall of the White Building. The stones wave and give off an iridescent sheen, as if they are coated with mother of pearl. They're so weathered they look like they've been there since the beginning of time. Maybe they have. The wall itself is so huge I can't see the top. But the archway is narrow and only a bit taller than Shvara Lohana. It isn't the stones' color or the archway that holds my attention, though. It's the Lohana wisdom formulas carved into the stones.

My Goddess leads me to the shimmering wall. She holds her delicate hands a few inches from the stone and invites me to do the same. This is the closest I've been to her, and to my surprise, I am filled with knowledge instead of desire. Dust cascades into the archway as my own wisdom formulas etch themselves into the wall. Four equations and my name inscribe themselves into the stone. What a moment this is! And although I don't remember how I wrote my formulas, I do understand their wisdom.

My Goddess gave me counsel for the wisdom formulas I wrote during my lifetime. She allowed me to go to earth and then to return here. Like children, we go out to have adventures in the world. It is a privilege and worth the difficulty. But know that the benevolent kingdom to which I have returned lies beyond the dream of the world.

As the stone dust clears from the archway, Shvara confers on me a blessing. Hotep! Hotep! In the area of my third eye, I have a satisfaction so mystical there are no words to describe it. I can't help but call out to her in return, Hotep!

Now I hear it—the voices of my tribe, thousands of familiar beatific voices, coming from inside the archway. They're singing praise to me. This praise isn't a vain thing. It's praise for my soul that has made the human journey and praise for my return home. Memories, forgotten memories of my spiritual family, are waking up, beckoning me into the archway. Their song pulls me into the passageway and as I enter, the light in the archway obliterates my vision. The only thing that exists for me is the chorus of mystical voices. I do not see them; I only hear my tribe's joyful singing welcoming me back, like Mahler's Eighth.

What? Mahler's Eighth? What kind of clue was Billy giving me now? Had Gustav Mahler written an eighth symphony? And if so, what did it have to do with the singing of Billy's tribe?

My pulse was speeding as I searched the Internet for answers. When I found a YouTube video of the finale of Mahler's Eighth Symphony, the *Chorus Mysticus*, I clicked the play button.

A chorus of hundreds of celestial voices was singing exquisite music filled with light. I looked back at Billy's notes. "The only thing that exists for me is the chorus of mystical voices . . . welcoming me back, like in Mahler's Eighth."

I went out on my deck and played *Chorus Mysticus* over and over. As I listened to the music, I was also somehow hearing the beauty of the voices from Billy's realm through my crown chakra. As the two choruses blended inside me, I spun off into a mystical realm somewhere between Billy's world and mine.

Billy's leading me to Mahler's Eighth Symphony was the cosmic crescendo of our communication, the supreme manifestation of Billy's world in mine.

After half an hour of this splendor, I began reading the lyrics of *Chorus Mysticus* moving across the video:

All that is temporary is merely an image
That which is unattainable
Here becomes possible
The indescribable
Here it takes place
The eternal-feminine
Draws us on high
Eternal eternal

How could this be? The words fit Billy's story as much as the music!

I learned that *Chorus Mysticus*, the finale to Mahler's Eighth, is played as Faust is welcomed into heaven. And although Faust lost his struggle with the devil, and although his journey had taken him far from what most people consider a spiritual life, in the end it was because of his struggle that the angels were able to carry his soul to heaven.

I could feel Billy smiling. My brother had brought me to this story to solve the most perplexing question I had about what was happening to him. How could Billy go to such a high place in the afterlife when the end of his life was full of darkness and despair? Like Faust, he lost his struggle with a powerful demon—his addictions. Now Billy was letting me know it was okay that he struggled; it was a Divine struggle.

THIRTY-FOUR

Golden Lotus Cave

A few days later, still soaring from Mahler's Eighth Symphony, I re-read Billy's last set of notes. Hotep? What was that?

Once again, Billy had transmitted a word I'd never heard of but which had ancient historical meaning. Hotep, it turns out, is the first word of *The Ancient Egyptian Offering Formula*, a blessing bestowed upon the deceased in the afterlife. Hotep prepares the soul to partake of the divine nectar of the gods.

Unable to sleep as the full moon lit up the dark world, I stepped out into the night air to find Billy waiting.

As the voices of my tribe faded and my vision returned, I was surprised to find that instead of being led into the White Building I was standing in a field of red and purple roses. But Annie, you've never seen roses like these. The neon-bright flower blooms are ten times bigger than the ones you have on earth, and they're so alive you can actually see them growing.

For the first time since I met her, Shvara Lohana isn't with me. I'm okay with that, though, because I hear her singing from across the rose field. There's some kind of dew falling on the flowers and also on me. We're being bathed in the mystical perfume of my Goddess. The roses look like they're dancing as their petals open wider to take in her fragrance. I probably also look like I'm dancing as I follow Shvara's voice through the glistening field.

Up ahead, I notice a golden dome of light. As I get closer, I see that it's a cave. Pictures of blossoms are carved around the gilded entrance, through which I can see my Goddess waiting for me inside.

Shvara is floating above a circle of golden lotus buds that sit on a quiet pond. True to her female nature, the love of my eternal life has changed her outfit. She's wearing a golden gown, sheer enough for me to see a hint of her body underneath. I'll never get used to her presence or her beauty. Her half-closed eyes make her look dreamy and seductive. If I didn't know better, I'd say she's flirting with me.

Once inside the cave, I'm so intoxicated by Shvara's sacred perfume I have to lie down. Up close I can see that instead of water the lotus pond is filled with milky nectar.

Shvara Lohana's eyes spring wide open and she begins a sacred dance. She turns slowly, and when she circles back, she's holding a violet flame. Her hips sway back and forth and sparks fly as the fire flows from one hand to the other. Each movement of Shvara's body satisfies a longing so much a part of me I didn't even know it existed. As my Goddess dances, there is no pleasure in the Universe that remains unknown to me, or unfulfilled.

Shvara swoops down and chants something over each lotus bud. Eight golden flowers open one by one. At the heart of each blossom is a flame of some shade of purple or red. These are the flames of my past lives.

People on earth are curious about their past lives. They want to know who they were, what they did, and who they did it with. I'm content just to watch the flames of my lives illuminate the golden petals of their lotus flowers.

Shvara flies to the center of the circle of flowers, and with her ruby mouth pressed against the milky water, she chants:

The bigger the lotus
The deeper the mud
The bigger the lotus
The deeper the mud

A solitary bud, bigger than the others, rises from down inside the pond. I'm surprised. This bud is covered with mud. I haven't seen dirt of any kind on this side of things. The muddy flower quivers and blooms in the golden light of the cave. As Shvara pours the violet flame of my last life into its heart, the muddy crust evaporates. The petals of all the lotuses start moving like speeded-up hummingbird wings. They swirl and collide and become pure flashes of energy as the golden flowers of my lives blow apart. I am witnessing the ceremony that will end the cycle of my being born.

Shvara rises from the smoky explosion, gorgeous as ever. She offers me a cup filled with the milky nectar of the pond. It tastes so unfamiliar it's difficult to drink.

It's sweet but surprisingly pungent. You could never drink this elixir if you weren't ready. I am barely ready, but I drink.

As the smoke cloud reaches the top of the cave, it forms a golden dragon with fiery eyes. He's fierce, but I'm not at all afraid. The dragon's devotion to me is obvious. He's my dragon the way Shvara is my Goddess.

My dragon has served me through my many lives. My protector came to me in different forms: a beloved pet, an unexpected stroke of luck, the kind act of a stranger, a chance meeting that brought good fortune, the friend who showed up when I needed one—these were expressions of his devotion.

I feel such profound gratitude I want to honor him in some way. I pour the nectar from the cup into my hand and offer it. As my dragon drinks, I am overcome by a longing. This moment is one I would like to hold onto.

My faithful dragon bows his head, touches his forehead to mine, and in a wild selfless act of courage he breaks open the cave and destroys it with his power. Then my dragon disappears like rising smoke.

I am now standing before the great emptiness of the Absolute. I am ready to enter the Void.

But, before I go on, I want to tell you this:

Life is a Divine mysterious impulse to be tasted and then released. Although everything in your life is destined to change, I wish that the sweetness of the celestial elixir you and I have shared will forever remain on your lips.

I took on form to enter time. I entered time to partake in creation. Since my destination is no longer the earthly realms, I will now enter the great Void and travel beyond time.

Shvara takes my hand and we ascend through profound darkness. As my Goddess lets go, I'm propelled into the Void. I am going beyond creation—before the manifest—outside of time. I am entering a world of non-existence—no light, no sound, no beingness. I have tasted the elixir and there is no fear.

This dark passage is leading me away from the earthly world and all the levels of the afterlife that I have traveled through. I am going from somewhere to somewhere else and I will never return.

I am becoming the Allness in the Nothing.

The raindrop is returning to the ocean, but there is no ocean, there is nothingness. Do not be sad, for as I am nothingness, I am also everything: I am the Universe, I am light, I am Lohana, I am soul, I am a king, a drug addict, a saint, and a beggar.

I am the Allness in the Nothing, the Nothing in the Allness. That's what the Divine is—everything and nothing.

I was born and died many times, and although I will not return, I have returned because I am everything that ever was and ever will be. I am the suffering, I am the grace, I am the truth, I am the play, the player, the scenery, the director, and the audience. And just as the shadow can never be the light, the story I tell can never be the Supreme Truth, but perhaps through these pages there can be a momentary taste of the elixir of eternity.

When Billy said "I am going from somewhere to somewhere else and I will never return," it occurred to me that he was saying goodbye.

Walking by the bay at sunrise, I could feel Billy everywhere—in the gentle spring breeze, the blossoming trees, the blue-gray water. His spirit was all around me, but something was different. I whispered his name, but there was no answer. I didn't have access to him.

I was frightened. Billy had become so much a part of my life. He was my teacher, the light on my path. It had become normal to hear him talking to me, joking around, giving me big brotherly advice. Then, I heard his voice from very far away. . .*I will never leave you.*

I got in my car and drove to the ocean, hoping its vast expanse would comfort me and make me feel closer to Billy. I stood before the breaking waves and heard Billy again: *I will never leave you* . . . and then he was gone.

There were so many more things I wanted to talk to him about, so much more I wanted to learn. I tried to taste the sweetness of the elixir on my lips like he had told me to do, but I couldn't. I wanted more.

THIRTY-FIVE

White Light Brothers

The summer seemed pale and lifeless. I tried to work on this book, but I was too sad. I wanted Billy back. People who knew about Billy were in awe of my experience, but for me the book wasn't as important as our relationship. And now he was gone for good . . . merged into the void of non-beingness.

Autumn came. Billy often said that nature is healing. I soothed my loneliness by walking in the woods, swimming in the bay, bathing in the light of the moon and stars. I began reviewing Billy's notes. How could I be sad? Billy lives in this book. He will never really be gone because he is now part of all that is, including me.

Late November, when the trees were surrendering their burnished leaves, just before sunrise I saw a thick ray of white light above me.

Good morning. Billy's voice was quite changed, its pitch much lower. I could tell he was speaking to me from somewhere much further away, but I heard him clearly.

A single eddy of light, whiter than any white imaginable, broke into the Void to pull me back into existence. Like an embryo in a womb, I again became the soul that lived all my lives.

The light ray propelled my un-embodied soul out of the Void and into a region where the light is so thick it falls like snow. I moved through this snowy light, the light that reveals the flawless nature of the Absolute, until I arrived at the present moment.

In the distance I see a landscape of snow-covered mountains. Standing on the white cliffs are shadowy figures, but the shadows are white instead of dark. The figures look as if snow is falling from their heads to their feet. I can't see the figures clearly. Their faces and the shapes of their bodies are a white blurry storm. Only their billowy sleeves and their hands are in focus. They are long and graceful, and rays shoot out from the fingers.

I recognize these figures although I don't think I've seen them before. These snowy shadows are Supreme High Spirits, who I will call the White Light Brothers. I call them brothers but there are females among them. And although these High Beings don't need to reap the rewards of an earthly existence, some of them have chosen to go to earth to bring the knowledge that something kinder, more beautiful, and wondrous is indeed the ultimate reality. Mahatma Gandhi and Martin Luther King were from the Brotherhood. Most of the White Light Brothers never go to earth, but their absolute light intermingles with and protects your world. If you focus on the white light, as you do my voice, I know you'll feel it.

There's an impersonal quality to these Supreme Beings, but that's not a negative—it's a big plus. There's a pureness to it. This is what I've imagined being in the presence of God would be like. You see, the Brothers aren't souls. They are pure Spirit. Just as our bodies are the carriers of our souls, our souls are the carriers of our Spirit.

And in this blazing whiteness, the whiteness of the Absolute, in this heaven of all heavens, I am about to shed my soul.

It isn't scary in any way. If you were inside a space suit, like the ones astronauts wear, even if it's the most fantastic, gorgeous, all the bells and whistles space suit, and even if you get to have wild adventures and explore unusual things that you've never imagined, after some time it's still a great relief to take off the suit.

Rays from several of the Brothers' hands reach out and join with my fingertips. I become one with their light, but oh, I want you to know, you must understand, that they are so most thankfully not me. They are so much more than me. Through them, I am becoming the first impulse of the Divine Source: Spirit. From pure soul I am becoming pure Spirit. And, as Spirit, I will leave the system of earth and all its heavens and go on to another Universe. I have cast off my earthly disguise, my life, my drama, my music; everything is being left behind, even my soul.

And as I go on to another Universe, flickering as a beam of light into the unknown, flickering as a flame of pure Spirit in and out of consciousness, flickering from being to non-being and back again, as I do so, I ask only these things. Play this role for me. Be the Scheherazade of my posthumous journey, keep listening for my voice, and always, always and forever remember my love.

ABOUT THE AUTHOR

Annie Kagan began writing songs at the age of fourteen. At fifteen, she was signed by a producer from Columbia Records. At sixteen, she was performing in New York City cafes and clubs. After ten years as a songwriter and performer, Annie returned to college, graduating with honors, and became a Doctor of Chiropractic with a successful private practice on Manhattan's Upper East Side. Attracted to Eastern spiritual traditions, Annie studied yoga and pursued an intense meditation practice. Following her inner voice, she left her career as a doctor and abandoned her hectic city life in search of serenity in a small house by the bay on the tip of Long Island. Annie returned to songwriting, collaborating with Grammy– and Emmy award–winning producer Brian Keane. Brian's high regard for her lyrics inspired Annie to join a writers' workshop. While Annie was writing her first novel, her brother Billy died unexpectedly and began speaking to her from the afterlife. She is excited to bring together her talents as a lyricist, performer, and healer in order to touch the lives of others with Billy's communications from the other side. She lives on Long Island. Visit her at *www.anniekagan.com*.